100 YEARS
of
COLLECTIBLE JEWELRY
(1850 - 1950)

by
Lillian Baker

Photography by R. E. Stambook

COLLECTOR BOOKS
A Division of Schroeder Publishing Co., Inc.

The current values in this book should be used only as a guide. They are not intended to set prices, which vary from one section of the country to another. Auction prices as well as dealer prices vary greatly and are affected by condition as well as demand. Neither the Author nor the Publisher assumes responsibility for any losses that might be incurred as a result of consulting this guide.

Searching For A Publisher?

We are always looking for knowledgeable people considered to be experts within their fields. If you feel that there is a real need for a book on your collectible subject and have a large comprehensive collection, contact us.

Collector Books
P.O. Box 3009
Paducah, Kentucky 42002-3009

Printed by IMAGE GRAPHICS, INC., Paducah, Kentucky

DEDICATION

To the Gem Lady,

VERA FRANK

who is herself

a gem!

Design and layout: Lillian Baker
Photographed by: R. E. Stambook
Art Nouveau Jewelry Casket: Louise Majors
Jewelry Collections on cover: G. R. Baker
                                Ginny's Antiques, Et Cetera
                                Manila Hoeck
                                Carolyn Vaught and
                                the Author

TABLE OF CONTENTS

SECTION 1.

CHAPTER I
INTRODUCTION

CHAPTER II
ALL ABOUT JEWELRY

CHAPTER I

INTRODUCTION

" . . . .On Arms and Neck You Make of Your Dreams Statues of Jewels, Palaces of Gems." (Victor Hugo)

This is a book representing one hundred years of jewelry, jeweled accessories, and "conceits" which are touchable, wearable, enjoyable, and collectible.

Each decade within this 100-year span reflects a subtle rather than a startling transition from one artistic period to another. The periods represented are:

Victorian	(1850-1900)
Art Nouveau	(1895-1910)
Edwardian	(1901-1910)
Art Deco	(1920-1930)
Art Moderne	(1935-1945)
Modern Jewelry	(1950-)

Collectible jewelry beginning with the year 1850, is not an arbitrary date but rather reflects the rapid changes in communications and transportation and the ability of factories to turn out material for a "new class" majority known as the "the masses". This mass-produced material included jewelry.

The dictates of fashion in that latter half of the 19th Century leaped the traditional wall of "high society" and dared to design the conceits for the "common folk". For the first time, the working classes were earning monies to supply the niceties of life. These included the most popular accessories, those which decorated the head, arms, and upper torso.

This is a book then, about jeweled conceits and adornments of yesteryear, (1850-1950), which have become today's treasured heirlooms and sought-after collectibles.

This is a new approach to the subject of collectible jewelry, sidestepping the "king's ransom" in jewels while aiming at the heirlooms of the ordinary citizen and the *nouveau riche*. It is a report of the conceits popular in the years when jewelry became a product for everyone.

Some of these jeweled memorabilia may be discovered in flea markets or uncovered in some trunk hidden away in an attic or storeroom. Desirable pieces are offered for sale at fine antique shops and shows or at exciting auctions.

The jewelry pictured on the color plates within the pages of this book represent collectibles priced within the reach of both novice and *connoisseur*. The author has deliberately steered away from those priceless pieces and *parures* which are coveted by museums or which lay within the protective confines of concrete or sturdy steel vaults.

This book specifically avoids examples of jewelry repetitiously reproduced in the many other worthwhile publications on this subject which are listed as an aid to the reader in the *Bibliography*. This study specifically focuses on the *neglected* items which contribute to a more varied, more unique, and more overall collection of jewelry and jeweled accessories.

1

The author, in attempting to bring to the reader as many examples of jewelry as possible, realizes that the variations of each example are endless. It would be an impossible task to picture within one volume the literally thousands of variations of a single theme or design of costume jewelry in the years 1850-1950. In many cases, the collector or reader will be seeing for the first time pieces whose very names would puzzle were not the actual items made visible in the color plates. Among these are sash buckles, swizzle-sticks, hair lockets, hat ornaments, bridal bouquet holders, and scent bottles -- all jeweled accessories long discarded or disbanded by fashion dictates, fads, or follies.

If there is a single truism in the study of jewelry, it's that there can be no dogmatic dating of pieces unless said piece is trade-marked, hallmarked, signed by an artist, or recorded in documents. Royal families kept explicit inventories of jeweled treasures as did courtisans or families of wealth. Wills endowing heirloom pieces are excellent sources of documentation. Marks signifying ore content -- silver or gold -- are in themselves little clues to *dating* a piece, but of no use as to maker or country of origin.

Very few of us can own a Rembrandt or a Renoir but it is possible to enjoy *reproductions* of the masters or substitute works of lesser genius. The same is true of jewels and jeweled accessories. The Crown Jewels and the "carriage-trade" collections glitter from realms far beyond the realistic grasp of most collectors; but there are lesser achievements of the jeweler's art to satisfy the demands of those with smaller purses and practical sights.

Jewelry and jeweled accessories, as with costume, are designers' fancies that become fads or legend; the fad fades, while legend becomes a legacy for future generations. But even passing "fancies" deserve documentation because they are a part of the human experience, and nothing better records "what fools these mortals be", than does the frivolities of fashion.

It has been agreed that fashion without jeweled adornment lacks luster, be it gold or mere gilding. From Biblical reporting to computerized projections, from savage to sage, the worship of that which glitters suffers few heretics. Neither have man nor woman ever lost their fervor or reverence for "that which glitters". False gods have fallen, civilizations have crumbled, rulers are lost in the rubble, but what have remained are the jeweled artifacts which tell us most eloquently of bygone customs and culture.

A more current example of the above may be found in the 1850 Crystal Palace bravo exhibition of the "Machine Age" which ushered in the Industrial Revolution. The mass-produced jeweled conceits which provided social status for the new middle class were on abundant display. The factory worker in the newly-built factories boasted of steel *beads* as well as the steel spanning-wire for bridges.

Apprentice-jewelers multiplied when the demand for their creativity came clamoring from the common folk as well as the royal courts and the "Upstairs" clan. Women from all strata in society began to *wear* their wealth, and *heirlooms* became as much a matter of pride as did *heritage*. Even the poorest farm-wife came to own a simple brooch or cameo; thus fond remembrance became the substance of which pure sentimentality was re-born in an industrialized age. And out of that sentiment grew the most popular of jeweled items: the brooch, the cameo, the ring, and the locket.

The history of jewelry was drastically altered when jeweled adornments were no longer the province of Kings nor the legacy of the Carriage-Trade. The Crown and Sceptre, once sacred symbols, were soon to be imitated and sometimes mocked. Women, once chattel of household and husbandry, exchanged their former bondage and became "slaves to fashion", finding the latter a more difficult taskmaster and more often impossible to satisfy.

Men, formerly decked in feathered hats suitably badged, wearing buckled shoes, frills, and waistcoats weighted with silver buttons and sundry jeweled vestments, soon paled next to their bedecked female companions newly blossoming in arrays of *aigrettes* and fanciful fans, with innumerable conceits dangling from *chatelaines*. (Then it was on to "bangles and beads" and all the other "refinements" of the new social order.)

To some, much of this excessiveness in decoration seems ludicrous and burdensome, but what has been preserved is gaining more and more interest for the collector who yearns for a bit of nostalgia, a conversation piece, or a coveted hand-me-down. For the collector, there has always been a desire to purchase a once considered trivial trinket that has become a cherished treasure.

This book seeks to enlighten the reader and the collector about jewelry pieces most easily acquired and more readily affordable in the ever-widening jeweled accessories offered at antique shows, antique shops, auctions, swap meets, flea markets, and thrift shops.

The jewelry and jeweled accessories pictured herein, with their current prices, should enable the reader to evaluate comparable pieces in the marketplace or in private possession.

Since prices on antique and collectible jewelry are based on artistic merit, personal appeal, and pure sentimentality, the fluctuating market values of a precious ore and/or gem has somewhat little effect. To substantiate this statement, one need only to witness the soaring prices of *Art Nouveau, Art Deco* and *Art Moderne* jewelry and decorative objects, most executed in "lesser" gems and base metals. This is not to suggest that luxuriously appointed pieces of Victorian splendor or Edwardian grandeur, (especially those with beautiful rose-cut diamonds and finely cut precious stones), will not bring higher prices. However, many of the exotic pieces wrought in "ivorine" (plastic) are bringing prices that would astonish the silversmith and gold merchant! The oddity of an *Art Deco* clip or an *Art Nouveau* pin in *base metal* can often bring higher prices than a low-carat, beautifully hand-wrought Victorian piece. It seems superfluous to state that *rarity* of an object would surely effect price, as does condition of piece and the geographic location.

"Jewels have always been a fascinating and extraordinary mixture of design and fashion, of money and craftsmanship, but at their best they are now more -- they represent creation unfettered, art as well as decoration." (Graham Hughes, "Modern Jewelry", Crown Publishers, 1963.)

3

CHAPTER II

ALL ABOUT JEWELRY

" . . .*the jeweler's merchandise symbolized man's love, man's achievements, woman's desire to enhance her appearance, the highest honor which can be granted by government, the symbol of emperors, kings, princes and potentates, but also a record of the economic ups and downs and the political leanings of definite periods."*
(Modern Jeweler, March 1977 -- 75th Anniversary issue.)

Nothing influenced change in fashion as did the social and political upheavals which seemed to arise with the Machine Age. Die-stamping superseded hand-wrought custom-made pieces of jewelry, and the scientific discoveries including that all-important harnessing of electricity, created an evolution in manufacturing and a revolution of peoples against traditional values -- moral and material.

The invention of the pin-making machine, (1832), brought about a myriad of devices to secure head and body attire. By 1850 the simple brooch was executed in precious metals and encrusted with gems and gemstones; by the '80's, there was a beginning emphasis on "non-precious" gems such as topaz, amethyst, and coral. And later there came the introduction of even more unfamiliar gemstones and materials utilized by the great innovators of the *Art Nouveau* Period.

Providentially for the jewelry trade, in 1849 came the discovery of gold and silver in America and two years later, Australian gold. These discoveries brought sufficient quantities of those precious ores for the booming jewelry commerce.

In the 1860's, the English firm of Elkington patented an electroplating process for coating base metal with silver or gold; thus, "pinchbeck" became *passe'* and the "nobility of the gems" was enjoyed for the first time by the "common people". This metallurgical discovery was perhaps one of the greatest contributions to the jewelry trade, for whether jewelry was plated or of imitation paste, jewelry was to be *worn*, not weighed for worth.

Exhibitions of great jewelers' works were a great influence worldwide, with plagiarism sweeping like the plague from country to country; thus, it's difficult today to attribute unmarked pieces to a particular country or cult. The piracy of jewelry method and design was common practice in every established firm; but there were still a few "eccentric" designers and jewelers who survived in their own right and were acclaimed both within and outside their homelands.

Most earlier pieces of the Victorian Era were imported from the Continent to America, but by 1849 Tiffany's founded their renowned establishment in America. By 1896, there were already 1,800 Trade-Marks of various jewelry manufacturers with established centers in Providence, Philadelphia, New York, Boston, and Newark.

(Providence, R.I., became the center of jewelry manufacture in 1800, followed by Newark, N.J., in 1912, with New York and Philadelphia treading the heels of the latter.)

In the 1850's to 1860's there was a demand for more jewelry than had ever been worn before by women, not only of *carriage*, but of the lower classes who were now being employed outside the household and in the factories. There was a clamor for cameos, coral beads, bracelets,

4

necklaces, earrings, brooches, and hair jewelry of all kinds. Lockets gained high appeal as receptacles for mementoes including a lock of hair.

In the next decade, 1860 to 1870, the marvelous invention of the sewing machine introduced varied costumes which women were able to sew rather easily, and it also provided the "ready-made" less-expensive garments from the factory. Naturally, the variation in costumes which the sewing machine allowed called for more and more accessories and gave leeway to a great many more fashions for all sects of the male and female population.

The opera, the newly established Shakespearian theaters which gained recognition in England, and the more respectful dining establishments which catered to *both* men and women brought in the era of cloaks and wraps, mantles and shawls, for the "evening out". These called for many clasps, most decorative in conception, center brooches, and many types of beaded purses since the outer-wraps provided no accessible pockets.

Fans and combs were very much in vogue, and jewelry for the first time was made available for *all* in matched sets or *parures*. The *parures* included necklaces, brooches, breast pins, earrings, perhaps a locket, a bracelet, or even a matched ring. The jewelry was usually gold or ornamented black enamel work with settings of garnets or seed-pearls, jet, and even human hair. Cameos were fashionable and were worn most often as breast pins. Seed-pearls were strung on white horsehair, and the twisted strands were made into necklaces or bracelets, earrings and brooches. The popular beads of the era were coral, jade and amber.

Human hair was braided and woven or twisted into watch fobs for both men and women and even into bracelets and rings. The beautiful twisting of human hair, which was coiled into the very sentimental piece of jewelry known as a locket, was placed under glass in fobs and/or lockets. A sentiment regarding hair was exemplified in an article in *Gody's Ladies Book* (1861):

". . .hair is at once the most delicate and lasting of our materials and survives like love . . .with a lock of hair we may . . .look up to heaven . . .and say: 'I have a piece of thee here, not unworthy of thy being' . . .".

During this same period (1860-1870), not only buckles and fastenings for shoulder-wear were common, but belt buckles of gilt, jade and mother-of-pearl. Combs were in their heyday and were wrought in almost every conceivable type of material: ivory, coral, silver, gold, and tortoise shell. They were nestled then with the style of the day at the nape of the neck above what was known as a "waterfall of hair".

Women replaced buttons with studs that had matching buckles and collar pins.

Black mourning jewelry was introduced by Queen Victoria with the death of the Prince Consort in 1849, and it was worn for *full* mourning periods -- the first six months of bereavement. And then there was a six-month half-mourning period when gray, mauve, or purple was permissible. It was Queen Victoria who set the standard of jet and black onyx for mourning.

During the middle sixties, the fashionable thing for brides was the coronet and filigree flower holders of silver or gilded metal. At the end of the holder was a ring into which a handkerchief could be slipped while the bride was shaking hands. That would leave one hand free to greet her guests.

The next decade, 1870-1880, showed very little change in the conceits for women, but into the arena of jeweled accessories came the young children. It was Kate Greenaway's influence in the very last period of that decade (1879) that influenced the dress of all youngsters. It required that they have "miniatures" of adult wear, and this included jewelry.

Men's jewelry of that decade still included the very heavy watch fobs but the chains were not nearly as *baroque* in design. Many of the chains had a flattened broader link, and were not only of gold but of silver and the popular gun metal.

The walking cane became very stylish and the handles were exquisitely wrought in ivory, gold, or silver. Shirt studs still remained fashionable and were buttoned down the *back*; soon there was introduced a new type of sleeve which required cuff *links*. Rings were in demand for the masses --heavy rings of onyx or with very severely set stones.

The 1850 *Crystal Palace Exhibition* emphasized the effects that the transition from man-made to machine-made had on the populance; it also reflected the influence of the women of that era: Sarah Bernhardt (International stage star), Empress Eugenie (France), Jenny Lind (The Swedish Nightingale), Lillie Langtry (The Jersey Lily from Great Britain), and Lillian Russell (The American Beauty Rose).

Men who influenced fashion were Charles Dickens, The Prince Consort Rupert, the fictional Sherlock Holmes, the eccentric and flamboyant Oscar Wilde, and the playboy Prince of Wales.

The influence of design in both dress and jewelry was definitely effected by the 1850 opening of diplomatic and trade relations with Japan. Just prior to the 1850's and the great evolution of the Machine Age, came the "peoples" revolutions in France, Germany, Hungary, and Italy, which produced political chaos; but out of those disorders came some semblance of order regarding the promises of a better life for the lowly classes throughout their lands.

The promise of this better life began with the Industrial Revolution in England and was followed by the influence of many Englishmen such as Oscar Wilde, who in 1870 introduced more vibrant colors into clothing, taking away the drab ugliness of street garb of the times. The combination of his influence and the collapse of the Second Empire in France, caused a more open and a much more daring influence in the vogue of jewelry and in dress for the masses.

In addition, inventiveness in transportation now made it much easier to bring the furs from the New World, as well as from the Hudson Bay Company's Canadian exports. From the boundless frozen plains of Siberia came the rare sables; from the Far East came the Persian lamb and the Angora. So now, with the transportation facilities, came the use of furs which had been previously reserved for royalty. A great many of these fur pieces were endowed with fancy clasps and buckles that often were accented with the jet jewelry which predominated the period.

Women of this 1870 decade wore earrings that were long and massive, always for pierced ears, and they were more noticeable because of the smaller hats which women were beginning to wear, hats that were decorated with feathers, lace, and other artifices. The small hat was tilted forward and set into place with two or more very lovely Victorian hatpins. Within another decade, fickle fashion would dictate enormous hats that shadowed the shoulders.

By 1880-1890, the Industrial Revolution caused Americans of the late

6

Victorian Era to be discontented with mere utilitarian goods. They demanded luxury items featured in the proliferation of budding publications printed for "common consumption". The new mail-order catalogues cultivated the small town housewife with the glamour of the big city which set the pattern for high-style and fashion trends.

Mass-produced costume and fashion jewelry have been shunned in most other published works, which is sad since this jewelry has a "noble" purpose; that is, to transform the "shop girl" into a Cinderella. The Carriage-Trade, catered to by Cartier and Winston, purchase the Rolls Royce of jewels while the "common trade" accept the mass-produced Model T's of the jewelers' art. And like the latter, early costume jewelry of this era has proven as collectible as the old "Tin Lizzy", for though jewelry was die-stamped and mass-produced, it inevitably came into the hands of the artisan-jeweler who gave it the final touch of his own creative engraving or improvisation.

From the late '90's and well into the turn-of-the century, the trend in jewelry and jeweled accessories epitimized the varying vogues of fashion, and utilized past designs rather than work new innovations. With the *Art Nouveau* artistry of the "eccentric jewelers", came the charm of new fashion and a passion for inner-creativity and inventiveness in design. Gems and ore were used regardless of monetary worth or popularity, and there was a never-ending lust to bring the shock of contrast such as placing common horn with diamonds. The aim was to forsake tradition for the sake of design, color, and texture. The newer metals such as platinum, chrome, and rhodium, fell heir to the station formerly held by precious gold and silver.

By 1910 jewelry became less *baroque* and much more dainty with cobweb, crochet, and lacework oftentimes simulated in semi-precious metals. But platinum was best suited for this fine work and was being used more frequently by the jewelry trade for wire and twisted filigree.

In 1910-1920, the vogue for low collars invited all sorts of pretty neck ornaments such as pendants, *sautoirs, lavalieres,* and brooches. it was during this period that the new innovation of a flat, circular, ornament was introduced which was the size of an ordinary medal and was thus called a "medallion". Workmanship was of such superior quality on these pieces that medallions deserve to be called jewelry. The name merely implies the *shape* rather than the decoration.

But most favored was the pendant which was often enhanced by being worn on black *moire* ribbon rather than on a neck chain.

Up to this time, gold was offered in green, pink, or yellow colors; but now the cool greys of silver, German silver, French grey and gun metal, plus the renewed interest in platinum prevailed in the delicate metalwork of the period.

The shirtwaist, of course, was "terribly voguish" at this time and the young ladies who wore them reveled in buckles and belt pins. The variety of such items was often bewildering and overwhelming.

The new cut diamonds were very much in demand in the beginning of the 20th Century, and they were produced in great numbers on just about everything from rings to brooches to cuff links, cravat pins, bar pins, hatpins, lockets, scarf pins and the like. Engagement and wedding rings became very popular in the very early twenties, and for the first time were enhanced from the plain to the highly decorated examples.

Up until the *Art Deco* Period, (1920), early craftsmanship shows the use of heavier electro-deposit on Victorian and Edwardian jewelry. It is most apparent that such earlier pieces were made to *last*, unlike much of the tin-like substances manufactured in today's mass-produced die-stamped costume jewelry.

"*The Studio*" magazine, London's monthly publication, (1893 into the 20th Century), was greatly responsible for the public acceptance of *Art Nouveau* design, and the influence of the artistic work pictured therein was felt on both sides of the Atlantic. What was rendered on one-dimensional paper was to be seen in all-dimensional jewelers' fabric of metal and stone. *Liberty & Co., Ltd.*, the London department store, offered mass-produced *Art Nouveau* jewelry, and the Bohemian, German, Italian, Danish, and French jewelers followed suit by crafting designs by the rare artisans of that fabulous *Art Nouveau* period.

At the *Paris Exposition,* 1900, the creations of *Art Nouveau* artists from America and the Continent were copied by the large jewelry houses. This early mass-produced jewelry of 1880-1920 had the "finishing touch", personifying the pride of expert individual craftsmanship. In the German town of Pforzheim, there were over one thousand jewelry firms, many eagerly copying the British and French masters, as well as the articles of jewelry from the major Italian center of Valenzo Po.

Art Deco, the rage in fashion beginning in 1920, was created by the discovery of King Tutankhamen's tomb. The influence of Egyptian design and motif is to be found in every maker's product, including metallic and glass objects primarily featuring the sacred scarab, the Sphinx, the Pharaoh, and Cleopatra's royal Asp. The interest in Cubism also spurred the use of geometric configurations conveyed in the new plastics, and in the plated metals of the Platinum family . . .chrome and rhodium.

The conceits of the new century (1900), and up to the years of the Great Depression (1930's), included the fan, parasols with very long handles, large combs and other accessories singing the praises of Oriental life. There were also muffs, handbags, and all the little trinkets that were dear to the heart of femininity such as flat cases of silver or tortoise shell in which to carry their calling cards and the ever-elusive handkerchief.

Hats took on new importance and were a mixture of many millinery moods which called for lots of ornaments including the fantastic hatpins of the 1900-1913 era -- the year in which the hatpin reached its height of popularity and its greatest *length*.

By 1903 there was wireless communication between England and America speeding the latest dress modes across the seas. This was a drastic change from times when the "Colonies" had to wait months for fashion plates to reach them by ship. The rapid pace was enhanced by the first transcontinental airplane flight from Jacksonville, Florida, to San Francisco, California, by R.C. Fowler in 1912. It wasn't long before new fashions could be speedily recorded from coast to coast. The desire for rapid communication helped establish a parcel post system (1913), which led to the very large mail-order houses. By 1922, radio was introduced into the home and the budding tabloids hand delivered the latest fashion news to even the most remote farming communities.

In 1933, gold was taken out of circulation and this naturally required a lesser quantity of gold in the manufacture of jewelry or a suitable and acceptable substitute for fashionable accessories. Enter full swing, the plastics and lesser metals.

Fashions barely kept up with the swiftness of communication, and today's vogue could become tomorrow's fading fad. The media of the silent movies created the worshipped "idols" of Hollywood -- the *stars* who were the real dictators of the world of fashion.

With factories turning out mass production, *original* creations were no longer the exclusive province of those in the "Blue Book". Jewels that were seen on the Silent Screen were copied and made available to many hundreds of thousands of "fans". The printed word in various movie magazines and tabloids carried enticing advertisements or movieland gossip, and taught men and women what was fashionable and where such fashions could be obtained through mail-order houses or in their own neighborhood department stores. It was this same mass production which naturally brought down prices and materials to meet the size of the general purse and public taste. And then came the automobile! At long last Nelly from the country could see *first-hand* what Nora in the city was wearing.

" . . .in the midst of wars and rumors of wars, women stopped to powder their noses . . .", and thus a "vanity" box -- today commonly called a "compact" -- became stylish. Formerly, such vanity items were hung from a *chatelaine*. With the growing acceptance of smoking among women, there came the cigarette case. (In 1914 it was still a misdemeanor for women to smoke in public places.) By the early thirties *costume jewelry* took the place of the real McCoy but was generally looked down upon by the "upper crust".

It was not until the forties and fifties that *fine* costume jewelry was near par with some of that produced by the most prominent and reputed jewelry firms in America and abroad.

Today, the term *costume jewelry* is a mere separation point away from the term *jewels*. The former is purchased by all strata of society whereupon the latter is usually bought -- not for wear -- but for either pride of possession or for downright investment.

The jewelry pictured in the color plates of this book is to be considered *costume jewelry* that is *collectible*. For the true collector, the investment in collectible jewelry is more an investment in past and future sentimentality, with the eventual realization of monetary worth when the collection reaches the marketplace once more.

*   *   *

SECTION 2

COLOR PLATES
With accompanying text, including
description, circa, and prices.

PLATE 1.

ROW & NO.	DESCRIPTION	VALUE
Row 1, 1.	MINERAL ROCK, Genuine amethyst stone showing how genuine gems must be *cut & faceted not molded*.	
Row 1, 2.	BROOCH, Silver w/gold wash, hand-crafted 3-dimensional floral set w/genuine amethysts. Circa: 1910	650.00
Row 2, 1.	CROSS, Etruscan-type, hollow gold, applied-design work. Circa: 1890	275.00
Row 2, 2.	CROSS & CHAIN, Old gold filled, set w/amethysts w/gold filled chain. Circa: 1895	350.00
Row 2, 3.	CROSS, Hollow handmade gold, engraved, set w/pearl. Circa: 1900	175.00
Row 3, 1.	WATCH PIN, Twisted wire, 14K gold. Circa: 1900	375.00
Row 3, 2.	BROOCH, Georgian-design work, gold w/drop ornamentation. Circa: 1875	325.00
Row 3, 3.	LOCKET, Gold w/applied floral design. Circa: 1880	285.00
Row 4, 1.	CHAIN, Double-strand, hand linked, 10K solid gold w/cabochon-cut garnet in clasp. Circa: 1900	750.00
Row 5, 1.	NECKLACE, Festoon-type gold w/cabochon-cut Persian turquoise w/ oriental pearls. Circa: 1895	1,250.00

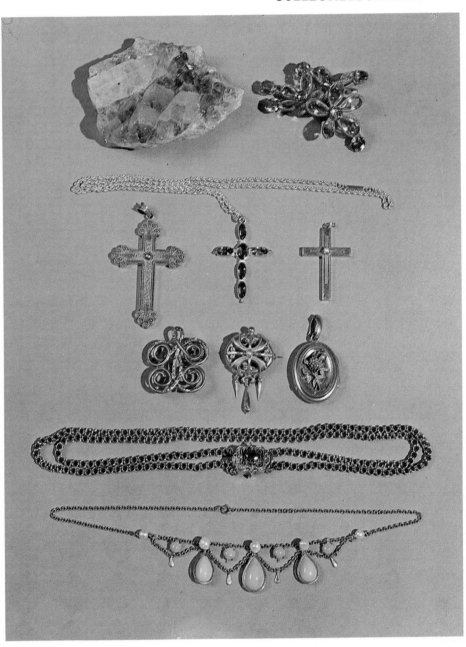

PLATE 1

From the Collection of: Vera Frank

PLATE 2.

ROW & NO.	DESCRIPTION	VALUE
Row 1, 1.	BEADS, Faceted French Jet, Bohemian. Circa: 1920	85.00
Row 1, 2.	BEADS, Cobalt blue, Bohemian. Circa: 1920	85.00
Row 1, 3.	BEADS, Venetian glass w/gold and mica flecks. Circa: 1920	110.00
Row 1, 4.	BEADS, Cranberry glass, Bohemian (rare). Circa: 1920	165.00
Row 1, 5.	BEADS, Crochet French Jet w/tassels. Circa: 1920	125.00
Row 2, 1.	NECKLACE, Hand-cut tortoise shell w/locket of tortoise shell. Circa: 1890	425.00
Row 3, 1.	BEADS, Bohemian ruby-color w/crystal bugle beads & tassels. Circa: 1920	85.00
Row 4, 1.	CIGARETTE HOLDER, Chrome and ebony wood. *Art Moderne.* Circa: 1930	125.00
Row 5, 1.	CIGARETTE HOLDER, Sterling and rhinestone w/original case (not shown) expandable. Circa:1930	95.00
Row 6, 1.	BROOCH, Wooden metallic thread w/Venetian bead tassels. Circa: 1935	35.00
Row 6, 2.	CHOKER, Filigree w/engraved links w/French Jet beads, Bohemian. Circa: 1900	85.00
Row 6, 3.	BEADS, Carved ivory, hand painted, *Art Deco.* Circa: 1920	185.00
Row 6, 4.	BROOCH, Filigree w/cranberry glass Venetian beads. Circa: 1920	65.00

PLATE 2
From the Collections of: Baker • Stella Tarr

PLATE 3.

DESCRIPTION   VALUE

Row 1, 1. BELT, *CHATELAINE*, Hallmarked silver, pierced, sculptured
& engraved w/needle holder and memo case, scissors
sheath and thimble receptacle (rare). Circa: 1895   750.00

Row 1, 2. BELT, *CHATELAINE*, Hallmarked silver (1895) *baroque*
seraphim and archangels: scissors in scabbard, *"D & F"*
(1894); pin cushion, *"L & S"* (1894); scent bottle (1894);
tape measure (1889); mesh coin purse (1892); pencil
w/retrievable point *"S. Mordan & Co."* (1894); thimble
(1895); and writing pad case *"CSFS"* (1892) (rare)
Circa: 1895   2,500.00

Row 1, 3. BELT *CHATELAINE*, German silver w/imitation jasper-
ware cameo w/filigree frame and mother-of-pearl chain
swivel. Circa: 1895   185.00

Row 2, 1. COIN CARRIER, Sterling hallmarked coin carrier and
powder compact w/carrying chain. Circa: 1900   275.00

Row 2, 2. COIN CARRIER, Engraved sterling coin carrier w/chain.
Circa: 1910   85.00

Row 2, 3. SET--SASH BUCKLE, SHOE BUCKLES & STUDS, Hallmarked sterling, box (not shown) imprinted: *By appoint-
ment to the King The Goldsmiths & Silversmiths Company,
Ltd. 112 Regent St., London, W.* Circa: 1895   395.00

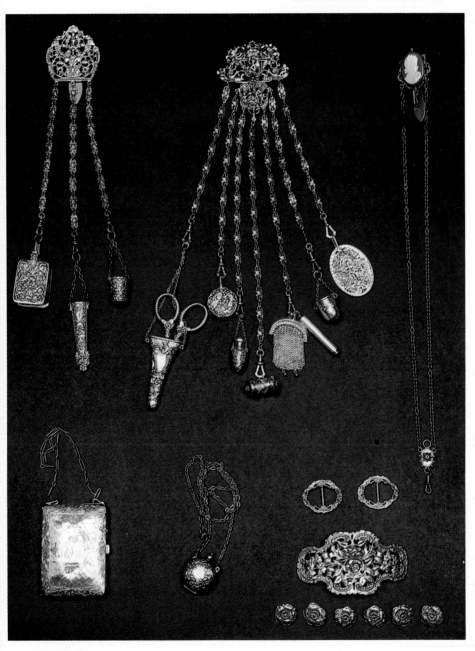

PLATE 3

From the Collections of:
    Silver Shop, Disneyland • J. Cook •
    One-Of-A-Kind Shop, Disneyland • Toombs
16

PLATE 4.

ROW & NO. L-R	DESCRIPTION	VALUE
1.	BEADS, Bohemian citrine color, marked "*Czech.*," finely cut and polished w/gilt findings. Circa: 1930	125.00
2.	BEADS, Bohemian blue-tone glass, finely cut and polished w/silver findings. Circa: 1930	85.00
3.	BEADS, Dark green seed beads, braided w/tassel, typical Venetian or Murano. Circa: 1920	95.00
4.	BEADS, Twisted white, blue, amethyst colors seed beads, high lustre w/Bakelite findings. Circa: 1920	250.00
5.	NECKLACE, Amber and jet color faceted Bohemian glass beads, (Czech.). Circa: 1950	175.00
6.	NECKLACE, Finely-cut amethyst color with glass ring inset w/gold enamel bead accents. Circa: 1920	225.00
7.	BELT, Crochet gold glass seed beads, 4'6" long, w/orange color glass tassel heads. Circa: 1920	95.00
Bot. Left 1.	BEADS, Double-strand faceted amber beads, (originally one long strand). Circa: 1920	185.00
Center 2.	BROOCH, Varied green rhinestones set in filigree mounting, marked: "© *Lisner.*" Circa: 1940	85.00
Bottom 3.	CHOKER, Crochet seed beads over wooden heads. Circa: 1930	55.00

PLATE 4
From the Collections of: Vaught • Baker • Warren

PLATE 5.

ROW & NO.	DESCRIPTION	VALUE
Row 1, 1.	CAMEO, Shell, 14K gold engraved frame, w/pendant loop, (Giovani Goto). Muses or lesser goddesses of the moon, and Phoenix bird. Circa: 1950	875.00
Row 2, 1.	CAMEO, Shell, low karat, filigree frame, w/pendant loop. Circa: 1895	175.00
Row 2, 2.	CAMEO, Shell, 14K gold ornate frame, w/pendant loop, (Giovani Goto). Very heavy and high *relief*. Circa: 1950	650.00
Row 2, 3.	CAMEO, Shell, low karat gold, heavy twisted ribbon cage. Circa: 1870	150.00
Row 3, 1.	CAMEO, Coral, sculptured and engraved gold, w/pendant loop. Circa: 1910	225.00
Row 3, 2.	CAMEO, Shell, full face, high relief fine gold *vermicelli*-work frame w/ pendant loop. Circa: 1900	250.00
Row 3, 3.	CAMEO, Shell, claw-set, gold w/pendant loop. Circa: 1910	125.00
Row 4, 1.	CAMEO, Shell, high relief ¾ profile, simple gold cage. Circa: 1910	325.00

PLATE 5

From the Collections of: Archer • Baker • Peery •
One-Of-A Kind Shop, Disneyland

PLATE 6.

ROW & NO.	DESCRIPTION	VALUE
Row 1, 1.	WATCH, Woman's lapel, (925) sterling and marcasites, (working condition). Circa: 1925	475.00
Row 1, 2.	BROOCH, Gold, commemorative of union between Germany and Austria, inscribed "*Weihnachten*", (Christmas); "*Gott Mit Uns*", (God with us). Circa: 1914	250.00
Row 1, 3.	WATCH, Woman's, dress-clip style, 15 jewel Swiss, (925) sterling set w/rhinestones. Note false winding stem to carry out charm of design. Circa: 1925	250.00
Row 2, 1.	BROOCH, 18K gold, center set w/ genuine amethyst, four *baquettes* and rose-cut diamonds. Circa: 1850	850.00
Row 2, 2.	BROOCH/PENDANT, *Pa'te de Verre*, signed: "*George Argy-Rousseau*," sterling w/gold wash set w/three cabochon garnets. Circa: 1910	750.00
Row 2, 3.	BROOCH, *Art Deco*, (925) silver, crystal. Circa: 1925	165.00
Row 3, 1.	BROOCH, Sterling, set w/chrysoprase and marcasites (Germany). Circa: 1925	175.00
Row 3, 2.	EARRINGS, Sterling w/emerald-color Bohemian glass w/marcasites (Germany). Circa: 1920	165.00
Row 3, 3.	BROOCH, Lalique-type camphor glass set in sterling w/onyx and marcasites, *Art Deco*, (Germany). Circa: 1925	110.00
Row 4, 1.	LAVALIERE, 14K white gold, *Art Deco*, chrysoprase w/diamond, frosted crystal w/pearl Circa: 1920	225.00
Row 4, 2.	LAVALIERE, Sterling, *Art Nouveau*, enamel w/mother-of-pearl teardrop, (Birmingham). Circa: 1900	350.00
Row 4, 3.	LAVALIERE, 14K Art Nouveau, w/opal and baroque pearl drop. Circa: 1910	425.00
Row 5, 1.	BRACELET, 14K gold and enamel links, *Art Deco*. Circa: 1920	250.00
Row 6, 1.	BRACELET, Sterling, set w/green onyx stones and marcasites. Circa: 1925	225.00

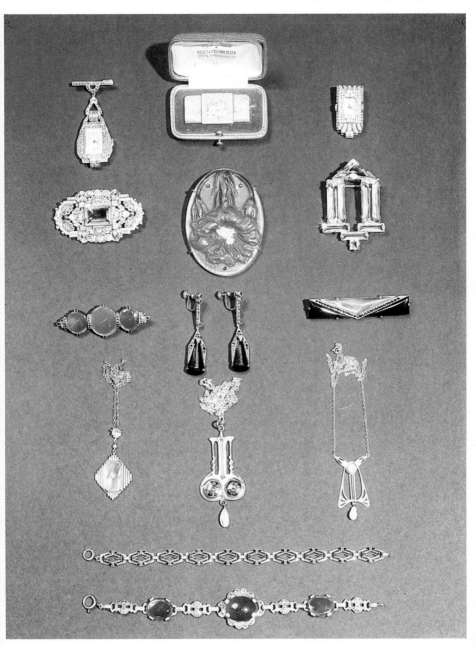

PLATE 6
From the Collection of: Antiques From Alota

PLATE 7.

ROW & NO.	DESCRIPTION	VALUE
Row 1, 1.	JEWEL CASE LOCK, Solid silver, finely-engraved border, large & heavy w/"secret" spring device for opening, size of U.S. quarter (rare). Circa: 1850	110.00
Row 1, 2.	LUGGAGE TAG, *Art Nouveau*, finely-sculptured sterling, Unger Bros., Newark, N.J. (rare). Circa: 1900	95.00
Row 1, 3.	CROSS, Sterling and jet w/glass bezel-set enclosure w/woven hair, mourning piece. Circa: 1860	165.00
Row 1, 4.	BROOCH, Jet floral mourning piece w/half pearl center. Circa: 1860	75.00
Row 1, 5.	BAR PIN, Hallmark sterling, 3-color gold; rose, yellow, green. Anchor denotes "Hope","...*which hope we have as in anchor of the soul*" (Heb. vi.19). Circa: 1880	85.00
Row 1, 6.	FOB, Key wind and toothpick, gold w/agate. Circa: 1890	155.00
Row 1, 7.	PIN, 14K white and pink gold, filigree w/2 diamonds, w/back bar for ribbon insert, inscribed "6-9-'23". Circa: 1915	150.00
Row 1, 8.	BROOCH, Heart-shaped, Bohemian faceted garnets in oxidized metal. Circa: 1900	125.00
Row 1, 9.	PIN, Clover-shape, rose garnets in oxidized metal. Circa: 1910	85.00
Row 1, 10.	WATCH PIN, Gold, enamel w/pearl. Circa: 1910	110.00
Row 2, 1.	NECKLACE, Carnelian and marcasite in sterling (France). Circa: 1925	325.00
Row 3, 1.	BELT BUCKLES, Heavily sculptured and engraved, sterling. *Art Nouveau*, coiled snakes' mouths join around cabochon garnet. Circa 1910	135.00
Row 3, 2.	NECKLACE, Venetian Peking glass and enamel on sterling. Circa: 1920	110.00
Row 4, 1.	KEEPSAKE PENDANT/CHAIN, Gold-filled box-link chain w/bezel-set convex glass for coin, pressed flower, or hair. (Spectacle is silver dollar size). Circa: 1910	125.00
Row 5, 1.	BRACELET, Gilt over brass, coiled asp snake w/cut Bohemian garnet eyes. Circa: 1920	75.00
Row 5, 2. L-R	HATPIN, Sterling w/cabochon "Dragon's Breath" stone, bezel-set. Circa: 1910	65.00
Row 5, 3.	EARRINGS W/MATCHING RING, Pink gold w/filigree, w/old mine diamonds; earrings w/European snap-close studs. Circa: 1850	Set 750.00
Row 5, 4.	RING, Dinner ring, *Marquise* design, *pave'* set w/24 rose-cut diamonds in Roman gold. Circa: 1900	650.00
Row 5, 5. L-R	RING, White and yellow gold w/claw-set old mine diamond. Circa: 1900	475.00
Row 5, 6.	RING, Sterling, Art Deco, marcasites and Swiss lapis, (dyed jasper). Circa: 1925	185.00
Row 5, 7.	RING, Gold w/half pearls and replacement imitation emerald. Circa: 1890	85.00
Row 5, 8	RING, Gold w/Persian turquoise and half pearls. Circa: 1890	225.00
Row 5, 9. L-R	RING, Gold w/claw-set ruby doublet. Circa: 1900	125.00
Row 5, 10.	RING, "Dragon's Breath" in sterling. Circa: 1930	65.00
Row 5, 11.	RING, Gold w/cabochon-cut garnet. Circa: 1910	175.00
Row 5, 12.	RING, 18K engraved gold set w/emerald and pearl. Circa: 1860	550.00
Row 5, 13.	RING, Gold w/genuine emeralds and pearls, filigree mount. Circa: 1890	450.00
Row 5, 14.	BRACELET, Gold-filled bangle w/pink French paste stones, unusual clasp. Fine workmanship. Circa: 1910	75.00
Row 5, 15.	BRACELET, Peking glass bangle, dark green. Circa: 1930	55.00
Row 5, 16.	PENDANT, Rose quartz-color Peking glass for silken cord. Circa: 1925	65.00
Row 6, 1.	VEST CHAIN, Tortoise w/gold swivel-lock. Circa: 1860	275.00
Row 6, 2.	WATCH, Woman's sterling engraved, hallmarked in protective tortoise shell case. Circa: 1850	325.00
Row 7, 1.	BRACELET, (Same as on Plate 22 but shown as example of various clasps exhibited in this row). Circa: 1950	250.00
Row 7, 2.	BEADS, Single-strand *Mikimoto* cultured pearls w/sterling filigree clasp. Circa: 1950	375.00
Row 7, 3.	BEADS, Swiss lapis lazuli w/cabochon clasp set in sterling. Circa: 1920	185.00
Row 7, 4.	BEADS, 4-strand Venetian glass ruby red beads w/rhinestone clasp. Circa: 1925	150.00
Row 7, 5.	BEADS, Finely-faceted Bohemian glass rope of graduated beads. Circa: 1930	95.00
Row 7, 6.	EARRINGS, *Art Deco* Bakelite beads. Circa: 1930	65.00

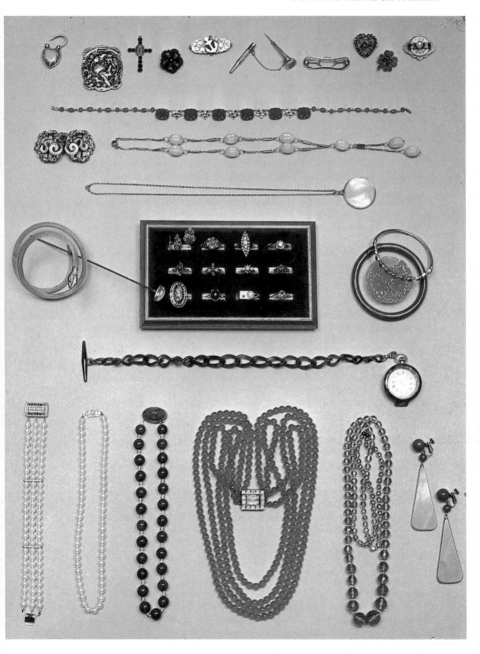

PLATE 7

From the Collections of: Baker • Majors • Vaught •
    Kastigir • Henning

24

PLATE 8.

ROW & NO.	DESCRIPTION	VALUE
Row 1, 1.	BROOCH, Hand-painted porcelain in gold bead frame. Circa: 1875	150.00
Row 1, 2.	BROOCH, Decal on Limoges porcelain, set in brass frame. Circa: 1935	75.00
Row 1, 3.	BROOCH, Heavy gold frame, hand painted porcelain. Circa: 1890	185.00
Row 1, 4.	BROOCH, German silver, hand painted (badly worn). Circa: 1890	35.00
Row 1, 5.	BROOCH, Gold frame, ceramic transfer of St. John, porcelain. Circa: 1880	135.00
Row 2, 1.	BROOCH, Gold frame, hand-painted jet glass. Circa: 1890	165.00
Row 2, 2.	PENDANT, Oxidized silver, black enamel and mosaic. Circa: 1860	165.00
Row 2, 3.	BROOCH, Gold-plated frame, hand-painted porcelain. Circa: 1910	55.00
Row 2, 4.	BROOCH, *Cloisonne* set w/pearls and garnets in gold filigree cage. Circa: 1880	550.00
Row 2, 5.	WATCH CHAIN, 14K gold, ornamental flat link chain w/swivel clasp for watch. Circa: 1900	475.00
Row 2, 6.	WATCH, Woman's, 7 jewel, engraved gold case, Circa: 1900	325.00
Row 2, 7.	WATCH, Woman's *fleur de lis* fob, finely-enameled, (French). Circa: 1880	485.00
Row 2, 8.	PIN, Enamel on gold w/sapphire. Circa: 1900	150.00
Row 3, 1.	NECKLACE, Low karat gold, enamel and faceted bezel-set large amethysts. Circa: 1895	375.00
Row 4, 1.	BRACELET, 14K findings and slides w/genuine gems and pearls. Circa: 1930	1,250.00
Row 5, 1.	BROOCH, Cinnabar in engraved gold wash over sterling. Circa: 1910	75.00
Row 5, 2.	BROOCH, Cinnabar, engraved, sterling. Circa: 1910	75.00
Row 5, 3.	BRACELET, Large blood coral beads, finely braided. Circa: 1910	150.00
Row 5, 4.	BRACELET, Smaller blood coral beads, finely braided Circa: 1910	135.00
Row 5, 5.	BEADS, Blood coral, polished beads w/cabochon set in exquisite gold clasp. Circa: 1910	275.00
Row 6, 1.	SCENT BOTTLE, 9K gold, monogram, fine engraving w/*chatelaine* loop. Circa: 1880	250.00
Row 6, 2.	FOB, Belt fob, woman's Burger-Ball souvenir, brass sculptured. Reverse: Dance book w/pencil attached, inscribed "*Mariahilfer Burger-Ball Hotel Savoy 23 Feb. 1905.*"	125.00
Row 6, 3.	BROOCH, Citrine set in shoulder brooch for Scotch kilt costume, gold wash on brass (marked: T.O.C.) Circa: 1900	75.00
Row 6, 4.	BAR PIN, 14K gold w/polished goldstone. Circa: 1900	55.00
Row 6, 5.	SCARF PIN, Goldstone, Circa: 1910	35.00
Row 6, 6.	EARRINGS, Goldstone set w/pearl, screw-back in gold. Circa: 1920	75.00
Row 6, 7.	HATPIN, Goldstone, 9½" pin w/½" head. Circa: 1910	75.00
Row 6, 8.	HATPIN, Goldstone, 8¾" pin w/¾" head. Circa: 1910	75.00

PLATE 8

From the Collections of: One-Of-A-Kind Shop, Disneyland •
Peery • Baker •Toombs • Wasserman • Heller • Anonymous

PLATE 9.

ROW & NO.	DESCRIPTION	VALUE
Row 1, 1.	RING, Pinky ring, Siam silver. Circa: 1950	35.00
Row 1, 2.	EARRINGS, Pr. clip earrings, Siam silver. Circa: 1950	35.00
Row 1, 3.	BRACELET, Link Siam silver. Circa: 1950	85.00
Row 1, 4	BROOCH, Siam silver. Circa: 1950	35.00
Row 2, 1	NECKLACE AND EARRINGS, Mexican silver set w/turquoise, marked "*Hecho en Mexico Taxco.*" Circa: 1940	250.00
Row 2, 2.	2 BRACELETS, *TOP*/Sterling (.0925), abalone, marked "*Mexico Hecho en Mexico.*" Circa: 1940 *BOTTOM*/Abalone and silver. Circa: 1950	125.00 85.00
Row 2, 3.	RING, 2 BRACELETS, Indian design bracelets, (A) Engraved. Circa: 1940 (B) Set w/needlepoint turquoise. Circa: 1940 (C) Matching ring. Circa: 1940	85.00 225.00 110.00
Row 3, 1.	CUFF LINKS, Originally pewter buttons set into gold wash over brass frames. Circa: 1910	85.00
Row 3, 2.	BAR PIN, Engraved sterling w/cabochon imitation jade. Circa: 1890	25.00
Row 3, 3.	BROOCH, Man's, Scottish thistle design, worn on upper left shoulder w/kilt, set w/amethysts, gold and silver hallmark. Circa: 1860	150.00
Row 3, 4.	BROOCH, Hat or fur, double-prong pin, marked: "*Weiss*," rhodium w/glass lantern insert. Circa: 1950	85.00
Row 3, 5.	BELT BUCKLE, W/slide and belt guide, sterling w/gold horse's head and accents, marked "*Devlin*," (Stockton, Ca.) Circa: 1935	95.00
Row 4, 1.	CHAIN, Man's sterling chain w/monogram tag w/silverplated cigar cutter, bottle opener, stainless steel blades. Circa: 1930	110.00
Row 4, 2.	VANITY CASE, Sterling, engraved w/enamel (maker's name illegible), for loose powder & rouge inset, wrist chain. Circa: 1925	175.00
Row 4, 3.	PERFUME, Sterling, glove size or palm size, *baroque* engraving. Circa: 1895	75.00
Row 4, 4.	SWIZZLE STICK, Sterling w/modern chain (still being made by Tiffany & Co.) (*Watch for display only. See page 149 - Swizzle Stick*)	*85.00
Row 5, 1.	SASH ORNAMENT, Fine French paste stones set in cups w/gilt wire. Circa: 1915	75.00
Row 5, 2.	HAT BAND ORNAMENT, Jet and crystal color brilliants. Circa: 1915	45.00
Row 5, 3.	SASH ORNAMENT, French paste stones and French Jet glass. Circa: 1915	75.00
Row 5, 4.	HAT BAND OR SASH ORNAMENT, Fine rhinestone and gilt wire. Circa: 1915	65.00
Row 6, 1.	BEADS, Venetian black and crystal color seed beads in twisted strands. Circa: 1925	125.00
Row 6, 2.	EARRINGS, *Millefiori* beads set in florentine silver, (Italy). Circa: 1910	65.00

*Price without chain.

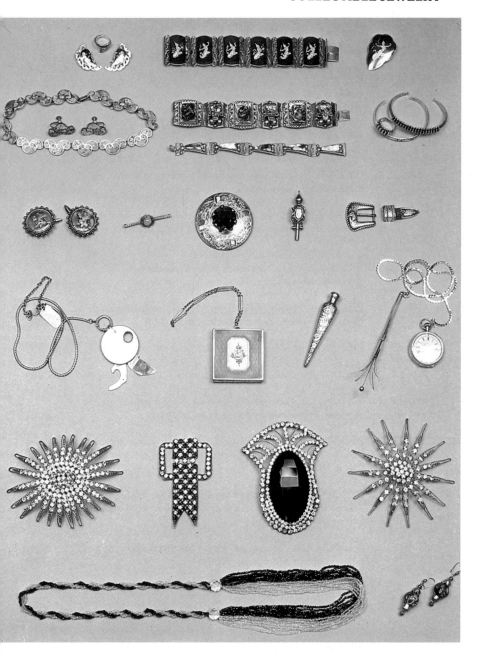

PLATE 9
From the Collections of: Baker • Majors • Warren • Vaught

PLATE 10.

ROW & NO.	DESCRIPTION	VALUE
Row 1, 1.	BAR PIN, Black onyx, cut & designed w/gold floral set w/genuine half pearls. Circa: 1895	225.00
Row 1, 2.	WATCH PIN, Woman's, 4-color precious gold set w/diamonds. Circa: 1875	650.00
Row 1, 3.	BAR PIN, White gold w/platinum top, filigree, w/small diamond. Circa: 1900	275.00
Row 2, 1.	BROOCH, Silver & gold old Russian-work set w/rose cut diamonds and drop pearl. Circa: 1865	550.00
Row 2, 2.	NECKLACE, Festoon, silver & gold old Russian-work set w/rose cut diamonds and drop pearl w/snake chain. Circa: 1870	850.00
Row 3, 1.	BRACELET, Cabochon and rose cut Bohemian garnets, low karat metal. Circa: 1900	525.00
Row 4, 1.	BRACELET, Hollow gold tubing, blue enameled w/ornate clasp set w/garnet & half pearls. Circa: 1885	750.00
Row 5, 1.	BROOCH, Enameled gold w/pearl center. Circa: 1900	150.00
Row 5, 2.	BROOCH, Scarab, enameled 14K gold. Circa: 1920	145.00
Row 5, 3.	WATCH PIN, Enameled on gold set w/genuine half pearls and bronze-color diamond center. Circa: 1895	275.00
Row 6, 1.	BROOCH, Red & white onyx cameo, set in hand-crafted Etruscan-type frame w/12 oriental pearls w/pendant loop. Circa: 1875	825.00
Row 6, 2.	BROOCH, Shell cameo in copper & gold sculptured frame, "Three Graces", set in swivel reversible frame for memorial hair or picture. Circa: 1860	525.00
Row 6, 3.	BROOCH, Onyx cameo, engraved, hand-crafted set w/4 old mine cut diamonds. Circa: 1900	850.00

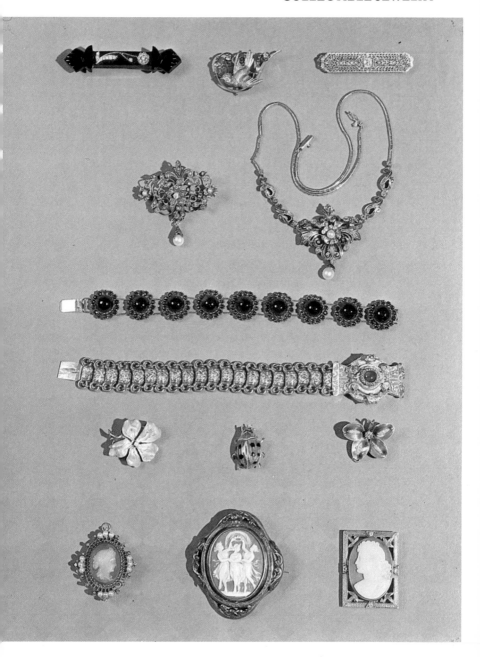

PLATE 10

From the Collection of: Vera Frank

PLATE 11.

ROW & NO.	DESCRIPTION	VALUE
Row 1, 1.	BRACELET, Sixteen 10K to 14K slides (1890-1910) w/genuine stones w/14K gold link bracelet, Circa: 1925	1,100.00
Row 2, 1.	STUD BUTTONS, Man's 10K gold, engraved. Circa: 1900	75.00
Row 2, 2.	STUD BUTTONS, Woman's 10K gold w/chain, enameled flowers. Circa: 1890	125.00
Row 2, 3.	TIE PIN, 14K gold bug w/genuine topaz, rubies, pearls, Circa: 1910	145.00
Row 2, 4.	TIE PIN, 14K gold, finely-sculptured Indian head. Circa: 1910	110.00
Row 2, 5.	CHARM, 14K engraved charm or medal w/inscription "1911 Winnipeg Operatic Society." Circa: 1911	95.00
Row 3, 1.	BRACELET, Sterling and enamel assorted hearts and lockets w/genuine stones. Circa: 1890	550.00
Row 4, 1.	BROOCH, Enameled child's dress pin. Circa: 1890	35.00
Row 4, 2.	BROOCH, Sterling filigree set w/diamond. Circa: 1910	85.00
Row 4, 3.	WATCH PIN, Sterling, Baroque cherub figure. Circa: 1898	85.00
Row 4, 4.	FOB, Sterling w/hair tie-string, skull inspired by Shakespeare's Yorick, (Hamlet). Circa: 1900	85.00
Row 5, 1.	BRACELET, Sterling and enamel asst. hearts and lockets w/sterling lock-clasp. Circa: 1890	495.00
Row 6, 1.	CHARMS, Set of sterling, hunter w/gun and African animal species. Circa: 1930	Set 165.00

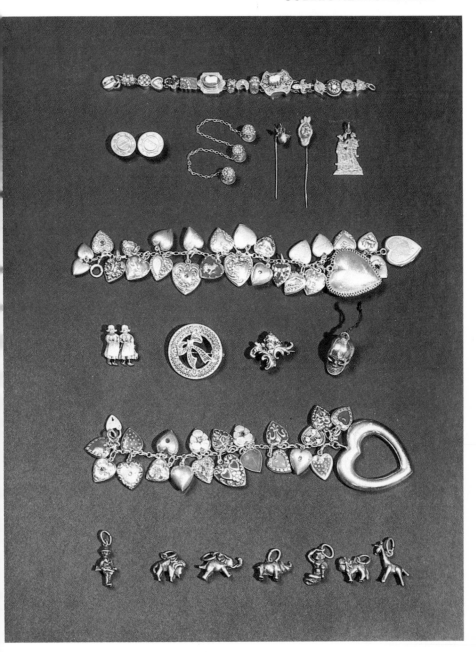

PLATE 11
From the Collection of: Peery

PLATE 12.

ROW & NO.	DESCRIPTION	VALUE
Row 1, 1.	SET: NECKLACE, EARRINGS, Hand-wrought, squash blossom, Zuni cluster turquoise; Circa: 1940	1,800.00
Row 1, 2.	RING, Hand-wrought silver, Navajo design rain-bird. Circa: 1940	150.00
Row 1, 3.	NECKLACE, Hand-wrought heavy silver, engraved w/Hopi design. Circa: 1940	325.00
Row 1, 4.	SET: NECKLACE, RING, Kachina, hand-inlaid in silver, mother-of-pearl, turquoise, coral, and tortoise. (Tortoise now "endangered species." No longer used.). Circa: 1940	Set 2,500.00
Row 2, Box 1.	RING, Hand-wrought Zuni needlepoint turquoise. Circa: 1945	150.00
Row 2, Box 2.	RING, Coral and turquoise set in heavy hand-wrought silver, Arizona Indians. Circa: 1950	150.00
Row 2, Box 3.	RING, Turquoise set in engraved silver mounting. Hopi design. Circa: 1950	85.00
Row 2. Bot. L-R 1.	RING, Turquoise set in engraved silver mounting. Hopi design. Circa: 1950	75.00
2.	RING, Zuni needlepoint design, turquoise in silver. Circa: 1950	125.00
3.	RING, Turquoise inlaid in silver, Arizona Indians. Circa: 1945	85.00
Row 3, 1.	BRACELET, Nevada-mined dark green turquoise set into engraved, hand-wrought silver mount. Circa: 1940	185.00
Row 3, 2.	BRACELET, Navajo, turquoise in heavy hand-wrought silver. Circa: 1940	185.00
Row 3, 3.	BRACELET, Cabochon-cut Persian turquoise set into heavy silver mounting, Gallup, New Mexico Indians. Circa: 1940	110.00
Row 3, 4.	BRACELET, Green turquoise set into hand-wrought silver. Circa: 1940	225.00
Row 3, 5.	BRACELET, Inlaid turquoise set into heavy cuff bracelet, Navajo. Circa: 1950	285.00
Row 3, 6.	BRACELET, Heavy twisted bangles w/hand-wrought silver setting for large turquoise. Circa: 1950	110.00
Row 3, 7.	BRACELET, Green turquoise set into engraved mounting. Circa: 1940	95.00
Row 3, 8.	BRACELET, Cabochon-cut green turquoise set into heavy silver mounting. Circa: 1940	110.00
Row 3, 9.	BRACELET, Silver engraved bangle, hand wrought. Circa: 1940	65.00
Row 3, 10.	BRACELET, Thunderbird design set w/turquoise, Gallup, N.M. Circa: 1940	185.00
Row 3, 11.	BRACELET, Zuni needlepoint in heavy silver, hand wrought. Circa: 1945	250.00

PLATE 12
From the Collections of: A. Fries • D. Fries • Baker

PLATE 13.

Top Row
  L-R
   1. HATPIN, 8" white pin w/⅞" gilt *Art Nouveau* mounting w/¾" oval
      aquamarine. Circa: 1895   85.00

   2. HATPIN, 9" white pin w/1¼" gilt *Art Nouveau* mounting
      w/ ⅞" molded coral-color plastic rose. Circa: 1900   95.00

   3. HATPIN, 9¾" white pin w/1" *Art Nouveau* mounting
      w/½" coral cabochon-cut stone. Hallmarked: "Sterling."
      Circa: 1900   85.00

Bot. Row
  L-R
   1. HATPIN, 7¼" white pin w/1" gilt *Art Nouveau* mounting
      w/⅝" turquoise color glass ball. Circa: 1900   95.00

   2. HATPIN, 9⅝" white pin w/1¼" gilt *Art Nouveau* mounting
      w/1⅝" pink slag glass/ Circa: 1900   110.00

   3. HATPIN, 8" white pin w/¾" gilt mounting w/⅝" peacock
      eye glass in crown setting. Circa: 1900   145.00

PLATE 13
From the Collection of: Baker

PLATE 14.

ROW & NO.	DESCRIPTION	VALUE
L-R		
1.	BEADS, Crochet w/glass ring and accent bead weights (Murano Mfg.). Circa: 1920	85.00
2.	BEADS, Chartreuse w/glass ring and accent bead weights (Murano Mfg.). Circa: 1920	85.00
3.	BEADS, Milkglass w/glass ring and clear glass bead weights (Murano Mfg.). Circa: 1920	85.00
4.	BEADS, Bohemian cobalt w/crystal color glass alternates. Circa: 1920	110.00
5.	BEADS, Carved ivory w/Venetian glass enamel overlay. Circa: 1910	325.00
6.	BEADS, Cut bone w/enamel w/amber bead separators. Circa: 1910	110.00
7.	NECKLACE, Bohemian topaz-color glass w/filigree, gold wash filigree links w/bezel-set topaz color glass. Circa: 1920	110.00
8.	*LAVALIERE*, Stone cameo set in 10K gold frame w/14K chain. (New Chain). Circa: 1880	150.00
Bottom		
1.	SET/EARRINGS, PENDANT NECKLACE, Marked sterling, (Israel). Etruscan-type craft. Circa: 1930	135.00
2.	*LAVALIERE*, White gold filigree, camphor glass set w/diamond. Circa: 1890	150.00
3.	EARRINGS, Silver mesh drops, screw backs. Circa: 1940	85.00

PLATE 14

From the Collection of: Stella Tarr

PLATE 15.

ROW & NO.	DESCRIPTION	VALUE
Top Left		
Row 1, 1.	NECKLACE, Blood coral, cut and polished. Circa: 1935	375.00
Row 1, 2.	BROOCH, *Satsuma*-ware, cream colored *faience*, decorated w/raised enamels, Circa: 1910	225.00
Row 1, 3.	BRACELETS, Six various shades of Peking glass. Circa: 1901	each 35.00
Row 1, 4.	VANITY CASE, Enamel on sterling w/carnelian and Ceylon jade. Circa: 1910	325.00
Top Center		
Row 1, 1.	BROOCH, Moss agate set into engraved silver frame. Circa: 1930	65.00
Row 1, 2.	DRESS CLIP, Cinnabar, marked: "*Made in China*". Circa: 1920	45.00
Row 1, 3.	BROOCH, Moss agate set into silver engraved frame. Circa: 1930	55.00
Top Right		
Row 1, 1.	BEADS, Carnelian, hand-carved, single-strand. Circa: 1920	165.00
Row 1, 2.	BEADS, Bohemian garnets, three-strand, cut and faceted. Circa: 1910	325.00
Row 1, 3.	BEADS, Ceylon jade, single-strand, w/gold wash over silver clasp. Marked: "*Made in China*". Circa: 1915	150.00
Row 1, 4.	BEADS, Fresh-water pearls and oriental jade, six-strand, opera length w/unique safety feature on clasp. Circa: 1930	5,000.00
Row 2,1	BREAST PIN, Carved bone. Circa: 1920	55.00
Center Left		
Row 2, 2.	SOUVENIR PIN, Sterling, replica pattern in miniature spoon given by jeweler to bride-to-be. Circa: 1940	35.00
Row 2, 3.	BROOCH, Sterling, die-stamped owl. Circa: 1940	55.00
Row 2, 4.	BROOCH, Sterling, die-stamped lizard. Circa: 1940	55.00
Bot. Left		
Row 2, 1.	GLOVE HOOK, Sterling, hallmarked English (pair of swastika charms manufactured in later years). Circa: 1850	65.00
Row 2, 2.	MATCH SAFE, English, Hallmarked, "*Sterling.*" Circa: 1905	85.00
Row 2, 3.	PENCIL, Collapsible w/chain loop, English hallmarked, "*Sterling*". Circa: 1894	85.00
Row 2, 4.	CIGARETTE HOLDER, *Art Deco*, silver and bone, original box marked "*Bernson & Hedges-New York City*". Circa: 1935	75.00
Center		
Row 2, 1.	PENDANT, Silver filigree w/chain. Circa: 1935	45.00
Row 2, 2.	NECKLACE, Filigree w/large faceted glass pendant set w/rhinestones, marked: "*Czech*". Circa: 1920	85.00
Top		
Row 2, 3.	SET: NECKLACE, BRACELET, Replica of Victorian pieces originally produced in jade and diamonds, now set w/Peking glass and French paste. Circa: 1925	325.00
Bottom		
Row 2, 4.	SET: NECKLACE, EARRINGS, Victorian reproduction in rhinestone and imitation emeralds w/2" blossom-shaped pendant in spiral design. Circa: 1950	145.00
Bottom		
Row 3, 1.	FOB, Man's watch fob in silver, an American Indian Portrait in high relief. Circa:1925	110.00
Row 3, 2.	WATCH, Woman's, Waltham, three-color gold w/chain and slide. Circa:1895	425.00
Row 3, 3.	BROOCH, Hand painted w/gold overlay and brass mounting, (possibly Limoges). Circa 1910	65.00
Row 3, 4.	PAIR PINS, Decorative dress ornaments, rhodium, w/imitation stones. Circa: 1940	55.00
Row 3, 5.	BRACELET, Sterling, marked: "*PAYCO Pat. 3-16-28 1/20-12K.G.F.*". Circa: 1928	75.00
Row 3, 6.	CROSS, Gold w/simple engraved design. Circa: 1930	65.00
Top Center		
Row 3, 7.	CROSS, Gold, highly engraved w/ivy motif. Circa: 1920	85.00
Right		
Row 3, 8	CROSS, Sterling, engraved w/ivy motif w/chain. Circa: 1900	65.00

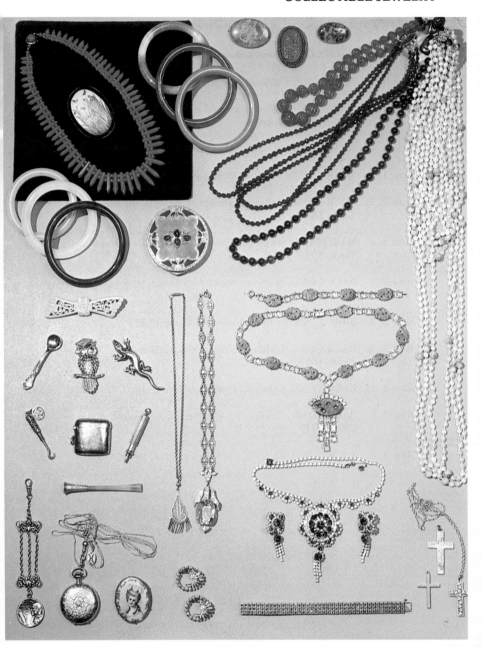

PLATE 15

From the Collections of: Biddle • Whittier • Henning •
D. Fries • Baker •Western Costume Co.

PLATE 16.

ROW & NO.	DESCRIPTION	VALUE
Row 1, 1.	BACK COMB, Large tortoise, (Spanish). Circa: 1870	175.00
Row 1, 2.	SIDE COMB, Celluloid, Victorian. Circa: 1890	55.00
Row 1, 3.	BACK COMB, Bakelite w/coral and gold wash filigree, Victorian. Circa: 1890	275.00
Row 1, 4.	COMB, Celluloid, French, *Art Nouveau*, Circa: 1900	55.00
Row 1, 5.	BACK COMB, Tortoise, Victorian. Circa: 1890	150.00
Row 2, 1.	BACK COMB, Bohemian riveted jet black glass, Victorian. Circa: 1860	150.00
Row 2, 2.	HAIR PIN, *Fleur de Lis*, French, tortoise, *Art Nouveau*. Circa: 1910	45.00
Row 2, 3.	BACK COMB, Imitation goldstone w/green stones (rare), Victorian. Circa: 1900	150.00
Row 2, 4.	SIDE COMB, Tortoise, Victorian. Circa: 1900	65.00
Row 2, 5.	BACK COMB, Celluloid, French, *Art Nouveau*. Circa: 1910	75.00
Row 3, 1.	BACK COMB, Celluloid, French, *Art Nouveau*. Circa: 1910	110.00
Row 3, 2.	BACK COMB, Tortoise w/jade, French, *Art Nouveau*. Circa: 1910	150.00
Row 3, 3.	BACK COMB, Tortoise, English, Victorian. Circa: 1890	175.00

PLATE 16
From the Collection of: Stella Tarr

PLATE 17.

ROW & NO.	DESCRIPTION	VALUE
Row 1, 1.	SIDE COMB, Celluloid, *Art Deco.* Circa: 1925	55.00
Row 1, 2.	HAIR ORNAMENT, Tortoise, *Art Nouveau.* Circa: 1910	75.00
Row 1, 3.	COMB, Decorative, Celluloid, French, *Art Nouveau.* Circa: 1910	65.00
Row 1, 4.	COMB, Decorative, Celluloid, French, *Art Nouveau.* Circa: 1910	65.00
Row 1, 5.	HAIR ORNAMENT, Decorative, Celluloid, *Art Deco.* Circa: 1925	55.00
Row 1, 6.	SIDE COMB, Celluloid, *Art Nouveau.* Circa: 1910	55.00
Row 2, 1.	SIDE COMB, Celluloid, *Art Nouveau.* Circa: 1910	75.00
Row 2, 2.	COMB, Decorative, Celluloid, French, *Art Nouveau.* Circa: 1910	75.00
Row 2, 3.	HAIR ORNAMENT, Celluloid, Victorian. Circa: 1900	65.00
Row 2, 4.	HAIR ORNAMENT, Celluloid, *Art Nouveau.* Circa: 1910	75.00
Row 2, 5.	HAIR ORNAMENT, Celluloid, French, *Art Nouveau.* Circa: 1910	75.00
Row 2, 6.	SIDE COMB, Celluloid, French, *Art Nouveau.* Circa: 1910	65.00
Row 2, 7.	HAIR ORNAMENT, Celluloid, French, *Art Nouveau.* Circa: 1910	65.00
Row 3, 1.	BACK COMB, Celluloid, *Art Nouveau.* Circa: 1910	95.00
Row 3, 2.	COMB, Decorative, Celluloid, Victorian. Circa: 1900	55.00
Row 3, 3.	BACK COMB, Celluloid, Spanish, *Art Nouveau.* Circa: 1910	95.00
Row 3, 4.	HAIR ORNAMENT, Decorative Celluloid. *Art Nouveau.* Circa: 1910	65.00
Row 3, 5.	BACK COMB, Celluloid, French. *Art Nouveau.* Circa: 1910	110.00

PLATE 17
From the Collection of: Stella Tarr

PLATE 18.

ROW & NO.	DESCRIPTION	VALUE
Row 1, 1.	COMB, Decorative, Celluloid, English, *Art Deco.* Circa: 1925	95.00
Row 1, 2.	BACK COMB, Celluloid w/French paste, Victorian. Circa: 1890	85.00
Row 1, 3.	COMB, Decorative, Celluloid, *Art Nouveau.* Circa: 1900	95.00
Row 2, 1.	HAIR PIN, Tortoise w/gold filigree, Victorian. Circa: 1890	55.00
Row 2, 2.	HAIR PIN, Bohemian wire-riveted jet glass, Victorian, Circa: 1890	45.00
Row 2, 3.	HAIR PIN, Celluloid w/paste stones, Art Nouveau. Circa: 1900	35.00
Row 2, 4.	HAIR PIN, Tortoise w/sterling filigree, English, Victorian. Circa: 1890	75.00
Row 2, 5.	BACK COMB, Tortoise, Victorian. Circa: 1870	275.00
Row 2, 6.	HAIR PIN, Tortoise and sterling, English, Victorian. Circa: 1890	85.00
Row 2, 7.	HAIR PIN, Amber, *Art Deco.* Circa: 1925	65.00
Row 2, 8.	HAIR PIN, Bakelite, *Art Deco.* Circa: 1925	55.00
Row 2, 9.	HAIR ORNAMENT, Double-prong gold filigree, Victorian. Circa: 1860	45.00
Row 3, 1.	BACK COMB, Celluloid, French, *Art Nouveau.* Circa: 1900	75.00
Row 3, 2.	HAIR PIN, Celluloid w/French paste, *Art Moderne.* Circa: 1930	20.00
Row 3, 3.	HAIR PIN, Celluloid w/French paste, *Art Moderne.* Circa: 1930	20.00
Row 3, 4.	HAIR PIN, Celluloid w/French paste, *Art Moderne.* Circa: 1930	20.00
Row 3, 5.	BACK COMB, Pierced design, celluloid, *Art Deco.* Circa: 1920	110.00

PLATE 18
From the Collection of: Stella Tarr

PLATE 19.

ROW & NO.	DESCRIPTION	VALUE
Row 1, 1.	COMB, Ivory, Oriental, Victorian. Circa: 1860	250.00
Row 1, 2.	COMB, Ivory, Oriental, Victorian. Circa: 1890	425.00
Row 1, 3.	COMB, Sterling, French, Victorian. Circa: 1860	225.00
Row 1, 4.	COMB, Bone, French, *Art Deco.* Circa: 1920	85.00
Row 2, 1.	POMPADOUR OR SIDE COMB, Tortoise, English w/*pique'* work and paste stones, Victorian. Circa: 1890	185.00
Row 2, 2.	POMPADOUR, OR SIDE COMB, Tortoise, English w/*pique'* work, Victorian. Circa: 1890	145.00
Row 2, 3.	COMB, Spanish, imitation mother-of-pearl; reproduction of earlier comb. Circa: 1950	65.00
Row 2, 4.	COMB, Decorative, French Ivory w/paste stones, *Art Nouveau.* Circa: 1910	65.00
Row 2, 5.	HAIR PIN, Tortoise w/14K heavy gold piercework, Victorian. Circa: 1870	135.00
Row 3, 1.	BACK COMB, French Ivory w/paste stones, French, *Art Deco.* Circa: 1925	55.00
Row 3, 2.	BACK COMB, French Ivory w/paste stones, *Art Nouveau.* Circa: 1910	85.00
Row 3, 3.	BACK COMB, French Ivory w/paste stones, *Art Nouveau.* Circa: 1910	85.00

PLATE 19
From the Collection of: Stella Tarr

PLATE 20.

ROW & NO.	DESCRIPTION	VALUE
Row 1, 1.	SET: NECKLACE. EARRINGS, Gold wash over silver, turquoise and coral inlay, filigree, (Nepal). Circa: 1950	175.00
Row 1, 2.	SET: BRACELET, PIN, Florentine gold finish w/simulated topaz and smoky quartz, marked: "Weiss". Circa: 1950	135.00
Row 1, 3.	BRACELET, Art Moderne chrome and sterling mesh. Circa: 1940	65.00
Row 1, 4.	BRACELET, Sterling Art Deco links. Circa: 1925	75.00
Row 2, 1.	BROOCH, Gilt on brass, simulated stones, marked: "Weiss". Circa: 1950	45.00
Row 2, 2.	SET: PIN, EARRINGS, Goldtone flower pin w/earrings w/simulated stones. Circa: 1950	65.00
Row 2, 3.	BROOCH, Reproduction of Victorian filigree butterfly pin, goldtone filigree. Circa: 1950	35.00
Row 2, 4.	SET: PIN, EARRINGS, Lapel pin w/simulated garnets, pearls, turquoise in oxidized metal, marked: "Czech." Circa: 1950	85.00
Row 2, 5.	BROOCH, Heavy baroque mounting, oxidized metal, simulated lapis, amethyst, turquoise, pearls, marked "Weiss". Circa: 1950	65.00
Row 3, 1.	BROOCH, Large snowflake, design rhodium w/finely-cut rhinestones claw-set. Circa: 1950	95.00
Row 3, 2.	EARRINGS, Rhodium and rhinestone clip-backs. Circa: 1940	55.00
Row 3, 3.	BRACELET, Rhodium, flexible cuff, exquisite workmanship, claw-set, pave' mounted rhinestones. Circa: 1950	285.00
Row 3, 4.	BROOCH, Rhodium, rhinestones w/simulated pearls. Circa: 1950	45.00
Row 3, 5.	BROOCH, Floral spray, rhodium w/rhinestones & simulated pearls. Circa: 1950	65.00
Row 4, 1.	PENDANT, Reproduction of Renaissance-type jewelry, "Czech", simulated turquoise and garnets. Circa: 1948	85.00
Row 4, 2.	CHAIN, 14K fine link gold chain. Circa: 1940	85.00
Row 4, 3.	SET: NECKLACE, EARRINGS, Bohemian glass, finely-cut and faceted beads, iridescent, exceptional clasp, tagged: "Weiss". Circa: 1950	165.00
Row 4, 4.	SCARF PIN, Rhodium tassels and pin-shank by "Emmons", reproduction mid-Victorian piece. Circa: 1950	35.00

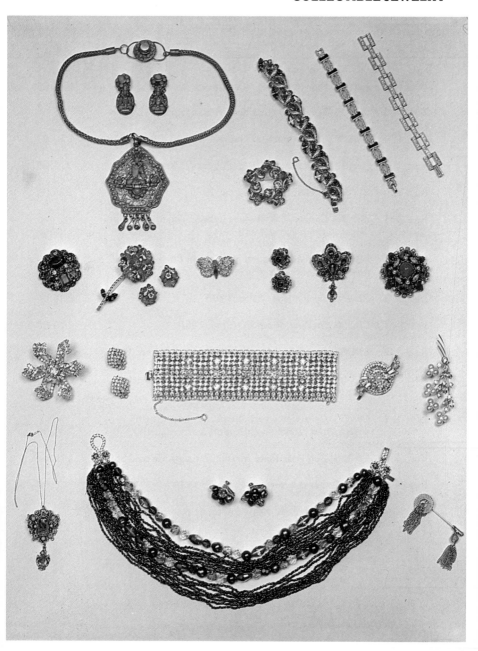

PLATE 20
From the Collections of: Alexander • Baker

PLATE 21.

ROW & NO.	DESCRIPTION	VALUE
Row 1, 1.	BEADS, Cherry amber, hand cut, (China). Circa: 1890	375.00
Row 1, 2.	BEADS, Bohemian glass and crystal. Circa: 1920	75.00
Row 1, 3.	BEADS, Bohemian glass and crystal. Circa: 1920	75.00
Row 1, 4.	BEADS, Cherry amber, hand cut, (China). Circa: 1910	350.00
Row 1, 5.	BEADS, 2-color amber w/gold beads. Circa: 1910	275.00
Row 1, 6.	BEADS, Amber, (Baltic). Circa: 1920	375.00
Row 2, 1.	BEADS, Choker, cobalt glass w/large cobalt accent in gypsy setting. Circa: 1930	85.00
Row 2, 2.	BRACELET, Red Venetian glass set in Etrusca-type mounting, gold wash. Circa: 1880	110.00
Row 2, 3.	BEADS, Ceylon jade. Circa: 1900	150.00
Row 3, 1.	CROSS, Sterling, (France). Circa: 1850	110.00
Row 3, 2.	CROSS, Bog Oak, hand carved, (Ireland). Circa: 1880	85.00
Row 3, 3.	CROSS, Filigree w/varied blue glass stones, (Spain), Circa: 1900	85.00
Row 3, 4.	CROSS, Gold piercework, Etruscan-style, (Spain). w/simulated cabochon-cut sapphire. Circa: 1900	200.00
Row 3, 5.	CROSS, Bog Oak, hand carved, (Ireland). Circa: 1880	110.00
Row 3, 6.	CROSS, Silver w/turquoise. Circa: 1930	65.00
Row 3. 7.	CROSS, Gold wash, filigree w/topaz-color glass stones. Circa: 1930	65.00

PLATE 21
From the Collection of: Stella Tarr

PLATE 22.

ROW & NO.	DESCRIPTION	VALUE
Row 1, 1.	WATCH, Man's very heavy, oversize, 14K solid gold, Hampton Watch Co., stem wind, stem set. Circa: 1887	1,250.00
Row 1, 2.	VEST CHAIN, Low karat gold heavy links. Circa: 1870	250.00
Row 1, 3.	FOB, Glass lenses set in gold spectacle rim w/pressed flower between. Circa: 1890	65.00
Row 1, 4.	FOB, Pink low karat gold, *baroque* w/escutcheon for monogram. Circa: 1870	65.00
Row 1, 5.	FOB, Watch, key-wind, pink low karat gold w/genuine bloodstone, (rare). Circa: 1870	95.00
Row 1, 6.	FOB, Tortoise-shell heart w/*pique'* work. Circa: 1890	135.00
Row 1, 7.	WATCH, Woman's Blauer-Elgin, 15 jewel, 14K, stem wind, stem set, hunting case, fluted edge. Circa: 1865	650.00
Row 1, 8.	CHAIN W/SLIDE, 14K gold, slide set w/pearls and rubies. Circa: 1890	475.00
Row 2, 1.	SPECTACLES, Woman's gold rimmed w/pin-on retractable reel chain. Circa: 1915	85.00
Row 2, 2.	HAIR PIN, 10K gold w/chain and loop at attach to spectacles. Circa: 1920	45.00
Row 2, 3.	SPECTACLES, Tortoise rim and gold w/hair pin, 14K gold chain. Circa: 1920	110.00
Row 3, 1.	LOCKET, Sterling hallmarked, engraved, w/sterling chain. Circa:1896	95.00
Row 3, 2.	PIN, Oxidized silver filigree photo pin, hand-tinted photo. Circa: 1925	25.00
Row 3, 3.	BRACELET, Sterling filigree w/French paste and marcasites. Circa: 1920	110.00
Row 3, 4.	BRACELET, Lava cameos, bezel-set in sterling. Circa: 1890	250.00
Row 3, 5.	BRACELET, 3-strand cultured pearls w/marcasites and pearls in sterling clasp. Circa: 1950	275.00
Row 3, 6.	EARRINGS, Faceted crystal drops w/sterling screw findings. Circa: 1920	65.00
Row 3, 7.	EARRINGS, Faceted amethyst-color Bohemian glass drops w/oxydized silver findings. Circa: 1920	55.00
Row 4, 1.	PEN KNIFE, 10K gold. Circa: 1920	55.00
Row 4, 2.	CHAIN, Watch or knife, 10K Roman gold. Circa: 1920	35.00
Row 4, 3.	FOB, Pocket watch chain attached w/retaining snap, "*Knights of Pythias*" emblem, gold on sterling. Circa: 1880	65.00
Row 4, 4.	WATCH CHAIN, 10K gold. Circa: 1925	85.00
Row 4, 5.	WATCH CHAIN, 10K gold. Circa: 1925	85.00
Row 4, 6.	WATCH CHAIN, 10K gold. Circa: 1925	85.00
Row 4, 7.	CIGARETTE CASE, Man's sterling engraved w/gold wash. Circa: 1920	175.00
Row 4, 8.	PEN KNIFE, Sterling w/nail cleaner blade, made by Gorham Silver Co., *baroque* sculpturing. Circa: 1900	75.00
Row 4, 9.	PEN KNIFE, Sterling w/mother-of-pearl inlay. Circa: 1900	35.00
Row 4, 10.	PEN KNIFE, Mother-of-pearl. Circa: 1900	35.00
Row 4, 11.	CHAIN, 10K gold, watch or knife chain, finely-engraved links. Circa: 1920	85.00

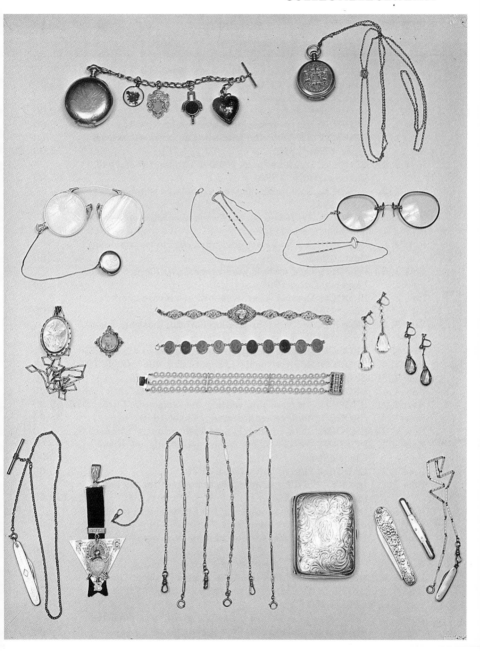

PLATE 22
From the Collections of: Hoeck • Kastigir • Majors • Baker

PLATE 23.

ROW & NO.	DESCRIPTION	VALUE
Row 1, 1.	BROOCH, *Art Nouveau*, gold wash on brass. Circa: 1910	55.00
Row 1, 2.	BROOCH, *Art Nouveau*, gold wash on brass w/simulated turquoise. Circa: 1910	55.00
Row 1, 3.	BROOCH, *Art Nouveau*, gold wash on brass w/genuine topaz. Circa: 1910	110.00
Row 1, 4.	BROOCH, *Art Nouveau*, gold wash on brass. Circa: 1910	50.00
Row 1, 5.	BROOCH, *Art Nouveau*, gold wash on brass w/bezel-set topaz. Circa: 1910	75.00
Row 2, 1.	BROOCH, Low karat gold. Hand w/filigree cuff and ball, Victorian. Circa: 1890	65.00
Row 2, 2.	BROOCH, Gold wash, filigree w/simulated sapphires. Circa: 1925	25.00
Row 2, 3.	BROOCH, *Art Nouveau*, gold wash over brass w/bezel-set amethyst. Circa: 1900	75.00
Row 2, 4.	BROOCH, *Art Nouveau*, gold wash over brass w/amethyst. Circa: 1900	75.00
Row 2, 5.	BROOCH, Gold wash filigree w/amethysts (large & small), bezel-set. Circa: 1900	85.00
Row 3, 1.	BROOCH, German silver w/cabochon-cut rose quartz. Circa: 1900	65.00
Row 3, 2.	BROOCH, *Art Nouveau* sterling portrait, (possibly Unger). Circa: 1910	85.00
Row 3, 3.	BROOCH, Brass w/blue glass stone, engraved. Circa: 1930	35.00
Row 3, 4.	BROOCH, Brass w/simulated topaz-color stone. Circa: 1930	35.00
Row 3, 5.	BROOCH, German silver, leaf motif. Circa: 1940	35.00
Row 4, 1.	BROOCH, Brass w/gold-leaf portrait under glass. Circa: 1930	55.00
Row 4, 2.	BROOCH, *Art Nouveau*, sterling and *cloisonne*. Circa: 1910	65.00
Row 4, 3.	BROOCH, Abalone set in sterling, Circa: 1940	35.00
Row 4, 4.	BROOCH, Blood coral set in gold wash mounting. Circa: 1930	55.00
Row 5, 1.	PENDANT, Molded plastic cameo and plastic link chain. Circa: 1920	110.00
Row 5, 2.	BROOCH, Pierced bone, Circa: 1920	75.00
Row 5, 3.	LOCKET/CHAIN, Imitation plastic tortoise-shell w/loop chain. Circa: 1920	125.00
Row 6, 1.	DRESS CLIP, Imitation jade set in Etruscan-type oxidized metal w/gold wash mountings. Circa: 1930	25.00
Row 6, 2.	DRESS CLIP, Finely sculptured brass w/filigree backing. Circa: 1930	25.00
Row 6, 3.	PR. DRESS CLIPS, Brass die-cast w/hand detailing. Circa: 1930	55.00
Row 6, 4.	DRESS CLIP, *Pavé* set simulated coral in rhodium. Circa: 1930	25.00
Row 6, 5.	DRESS CLIP, Brass, Etruscan-type beading and filigree. Circa: 1930	20.00
Row 7, 1.	CLIP, Hat or fur, double-prong heavy spring w/simulated aquamarine, gold wash. Circa: 1940	85.00
Row 7, 2.	BROOCH, Gilt on brass, ruby red-faceted glass, bezel-set as flower petals. Circa: 1940	55.00
Row 7, 3.	COMB, Hinged-clip side comb, decorative and functional, rhodium and rhinestones. Circa: 1940	15.00

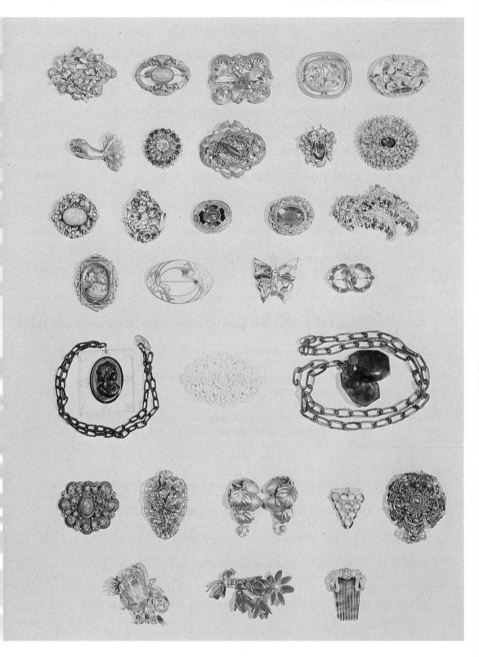

PLATE 23
From the Collection of: Alexander

PLATE 24.

ROW & NO.	DESCRIPTION	VALUE
Row 1, 1.	SCARF PIN, w/safety nib, gold plate, synthetic stone. Circa: 1920	25.00
Row 1, 2.	TIE PIN, Gold plate. Circa: 1920	25.00
Row 1, 3.	TIE PIN, "Made in Germany" unusual design, German silver w/synthetic stones. Circa: 1920	25.00
Row 1, 4.	TIE PIN, Gold plate, synthetic stones. Circa: 1920	25.00
Row 1, 5.	TIE PIN, Gold plate, half pearls. Circa: 1920	35.00
Row 1, 6.	SCARF PIN, w/safety nib, gold wire circular design. Circa: 1920	75.00
Row 1, 7.	TIE PIN, Gold cross, 14K. Circa: 1910	65.00
Row 1, 8.	TIE PIN, Unusual locket-type set w/photos, 10K gold. Circa: 1910	85.00
Row 1, 9.	TIE PIN, Gold Tiffany-type set w/gemstone, Circa: 1920	55.00
Row 1, 10.	SCARF PIN, W/safety nib, brass w/synthetic stone. Circa: 1920	25.00
Row 1, 11.	TIE PIN, Silver w/abalone. Circa: 1920	15.00
Row 2, 1.	BRACELETS, Pair of bangle-type, sterling set w/imitation stones. Circa: 1900	Each 55.00
Row 2, 2.	LORGNETTE, *Art Nouveau*, gold wash over brass, folding spectacles on long chain. Circa: 1895	325.00
Row 2, 3.	EARRINGS, Gold wash, made by Cartier. Circa: 1930	110.00
Row 3, 1.	SHOE BUCKLES, *Grosgrain* and French jet. Circa: 1950	55.00
Row 3, 2.	CUFF LINKS, Man's 10K gold, engraved. Circa: 1920	45.00
Row 3, 3.	BROOCH, Enamel in gold frame, religious motif. Circa: 1890	75.00
Row 3, 4.	FOB LOCKET, Man's engraved gold watch fob locket, red tiger eye cameo. Circa: 1920	75.00
Row 3, 5.	SHOE BUCKLES, Woman's pewter w/cut steel beads. Circa: 1900	75.00
Row 4, 1.	NECKLACE, Bohemian garnets w/gold chain. Circa: 1895	325.00
Row 4, 2.	NECKLACE, Sterling w/marcasites. Circa: 1900	225.00

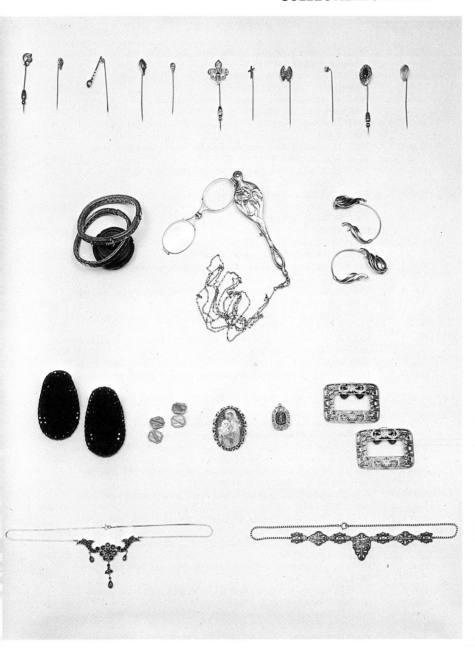

PLATE 24

From the Collections of: Majors • Lambert • Taylor •
Roth • Baker • Schemm

PLATE 25.

ROW & NO.	DESCRIPTION	VALUE
Row 1, 1.	WATCH, Woman's, English, 15 jewel, stem wind, stem set, silver, open-face. Circa: 1915	125.00
Row 1, 2.	WATCH, Woman's Swiss movement, 7 jewel, 14K gold and enamel, open face. Circa: 1900	250.00
Row 1, 3.	WATCH, Woman's hunting case, Marcella Swiss 15 jewel, stem wind, lever set, 14K gold, enamel dial. Circa: 1905	575.00
Row 1, 4.	WATCH, Woman's English, 21 jewel, gold and enamel portrait. Circa: 1900	550.00
Row 1, 5.	WATCH, Woman's, 14K gold and enamel, 7 jewel, open face, stem wind, stem set. Circa: 1900	250.00
Row 2, 1.	WATCH, Woman's 14K gold, Hampden, 7 jewel, stem wind, lever set, hunting case. Circa: 1890	650.00
Row 2, 2.	WATCH, PIN, Heavy gold, beautifully sculptured and engraved. Circa: 1900	325.00
Row 2, 3.	WATCH, Woman's, gold w/"Pie Crust" engraved hunting case. Circa: 1880	650.00
Row 2, 4.	WATCH, Woman's, Elgin, 18K gold, 15 jewel, w/"Pie Crust" engraved hunting case, stem wind, stem set. Circa: 1897	850.00
Row 2, 5.	CHAIN W/SLIDE, 14K gold w/cabochon garnets opal and pearls; slide w/52" 14K chain. Circa: 1900	525.00
Row 2, 6.	WATCH, Woman's 14K gold hunting case, Molly Stark model, Hampden, 7 jewel, stem wind, stem set. Circa: 1915	750.00
Row 3, 1.	WATCH, Woman's oxidized silver case, open face, French, 10 jewel, stem wind, pin set. Circa: 1890	225.00
Row 3, 2.	WATCH, Woman's Elgin, 15 jewel, hunting case, silver pie/crust, illustrated dial (stem set at III o'clock). Circa: 1875	650.00
Row 3, 3.	WATCH, Woman's, 15 jewel, Swiss, 14K case, open face. Circa: 1915	350.00
Row 4, 1.	FOB, Man's *grosgrain* watch fob, low karat gold, engraved pendant, set w/3 rubies. Circa: 1910	110.00
Row 4, 2.	FOB, Man's *grosgrain* watch fob, gold engraved, double-hasp buckle. Circa: 1920	55.00
Row 4, 3.	WATCH, Man's double-case, 10 jewel, silver, open face, French hand-painted porcelain dial w/oxidized metal protective case. Circa: 1850	650.00
Row 4, 4.	WATCH, Man's double-case Swiss, 10 jewel, openface, silver stem wind, pin set, in protective case. Circa: 1890	375.00
Row 4, 5.	WATCH, Man's, English, 10 jewel, open face, engraved 18K gold, key wind and key set w/key. Circa: 1870	750.00
Row 5, 1.	WATCH, Man's Elgin, stem wind, stem set, 7 jewel, hunting case, 14K gold. Circa: 1879	895.00
Row 5, 2.	WATCH, Man's, hunting case, 17 jewel, 14K gold, French, stem wind, lever set. Circa: 1900	895.00
Row 5, 3.	WATCH, Man's, Elgin, 7 jewel, hunting case, 14K gold, stem wind, stem set. Circa: 1870	895.00
Row 6, 1.	WATCH, Man's/woman's, 7 jewel Elgin, hunting case, 14K gold, stem wind, stem set. Circa: 1890	750.00
Row 6, 2.	WATCH, Man's/woman's, 7 jewel, Waltham, 14K gold, hunting case, stem wind, stem set. Circa: 1900	650.00
Row 6, 3.	WATCH, Man's/woman's 7 jewel, 14K gold, hunting case, Seth Thomas, stem wind, stem set. Circa: 1884	850.00
Row 6, 4.	WATCH, Man's/woman's, 15 jewel, 18K gold, Waltham, hunting case. Circa: 1890	750.00
Row 6, 5.	WATCH, Man's/woman's, 15 jewel, 14K gold Elgin, hunting case, stem wind, stem set. Circa: 1879	825.00

59

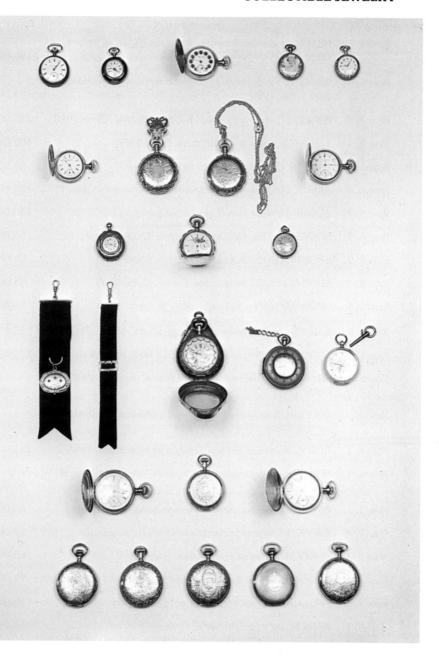

PLATE 25

From the Collections of: Majors • Ginny's Antiques, Et Cetera

PLATE 26.

ROW & NO.	DESCRIPTION	VALUE
Row 1, 1.	BRACELET, Gold-coil bangle, snake design, set w/garnets. Circa: 1925	150.00
Row 1, 2.	BROOCH, Finely-cut and polished Bohemian garnets set in 14K gold. Circa: 1900	195.00
Row 1, 3.	BRACELET, *Pavé* set garnets in 14K gold links. Circa: 1910	225.00
Row 1, 4.	EARRINGS, Garnets w/stud wires. Circa: 1920	100.00
Row 1, 5.	BAR PIN, Cut and faceted garnets. Circa: 1900	85.00
Row 2, 1.	BEADS, 10" long strand of matched-sized garnets. Circa: 1920	125.00
Row 3, 1.	BEADS, 12" long strand, graduated garnets. Circa: 1920	150.00
Row 4, 1.	SHOE BUCKLES, Steel beads, French. Circa: 1900	55.00
Row 4, 2.	SHOE BUCKLES, Steel beads, French. Circa: 1900	55.00
Row 4, 3.	SHOE BUCKLES, Steel beads, French. Circa: 1900	55.00
Row 5, 1.	BROOCH, Sterling and marcasite leaf. Circa: 1920	75.00
Row 5, 2.	BAR PIN, Sterling and marcasite, geometric design. Circa: 1920	65.00
Row 5, 3.	BROOCH, Sterling and marcasite, *Art Deco* bow. Circa: 1920	125.00
Row 5, 4.	BROOCH, Sterling and marcasite scarab, marked "1900". Circa: 1900	85.00
Row 5, 5.	BROOCH, Beautifully-detailed hand-molded and sculptured sterling. Circa: 1910	100.00
Row 6, 1.	BEADS, Bohemian-cut and polished jet rope. Circa: 1895	125.00
Row 6, 2.	BROOCH, Jet, mourning jewelry, set w/gold anchor (hope). Circa: 1890	65.00
Row 7, 1.	BROOCH, Jet, mourning, set w/marcasites. Circa: 1890	85.00
Row 7, 2.	BROOCH, Engraved jet, horse's head w/gold accents. Circa: 1900	65.00
Row 7, 3.	BROOCH, Jet, large oval portrait. Circa: 1890	65.00
Row 7, 4.	BROOCH, Jet, cut and faceted pair hearts in gold. Circa: 1890	75.00
Row 7, 5.	BROOCH, Jet, oval set w/gold and pearls. Circa: 1890	95.00
Row 8, 1.	BAR PIN, Jet w/pearls. Circa: 1890	165.00
Row 8, 2.	BROOCH, Jet, clasped hand w/mourning wreath. Circa: 1890	110.00
Row 8, 3.	BAR PIN, Jet. Circa: 1890	45.00

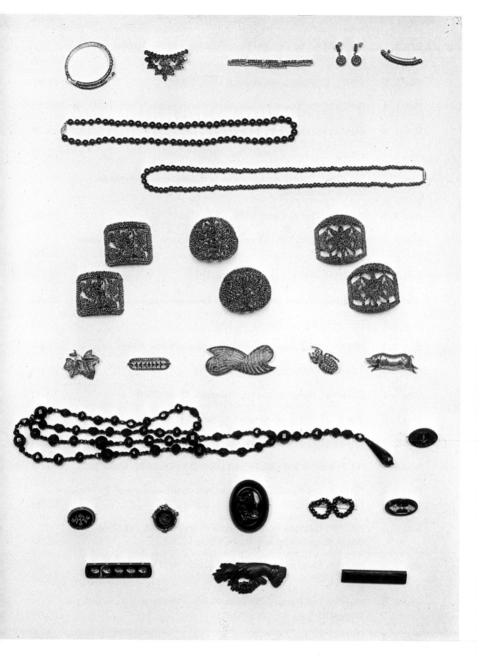

PLATE 26

From the Collections of: Toombs • Wasserman •
One-Of-A-Kind Shop, Disneyland

PLATE 27.

ROW & NO.	DESCRIPTION	VALUE
Row 1, 1.	NECKLACE, *Art Deco*, brass w/Bakelite beads and pendant. Circa: 1925	325.00
Row 1, 2.	TIARA, Celluloid w/rhinestones. Circa: 1930	75.00
Row 1, 3.	BRACELETS, 3-matched bangles of carved plastic. Circa: 1930 set	145.00
Row 1, 4.	BRACELET, Cuff-style, carved plastic. Circa: 1930	85.00
Row 2, 1.	BRACELET, Link Bakelite. Circa: 1930	75.00
Row 2, 2.	BROOCH, Carved plastic Scottie w/rhinestone eyes on plastic mount. Circa: 1930	95.00
Row 3, 1.	BAR PIN, Plastic. Circa: 1925	20.00
Row 3, 2.	BAR PIN, Plastic, scarab center w/amber color Phoenix-bird wings. Circa: 1925	125.00
Row 3, 3.	BAR PIN, *Art Deco*, plastic, Circa: 1925	55.00
Row 4, 1.	BROOCH, Carved Bakelite. Circa: 1930	25.00
Row 4, 2.	DRESS CLIP, Bakelite. Circa: 1935	35.00
Row 4, 3.	BROOCH, Polished wood and clear plastic. Circa: 1935	125.00
Row 4, 4.	3 DRESS CLIPS, Bakelite. Circa: 1930 each	20.00
Row 5, 1.	BROOCH, Hand-cut and painted wood. Circa: 1940	10.00
Row 5, 2.	BROOCH, Hand-carved wood. Circa: 1950	35.00
Row 5, 3.	BROOCH, Hand-carved and painted. Circa: 1930	35.00
Row 6, 1.	HATPIN, Brass and Celluloid *Art Deco*, (Egyptian motif). Circa: 1925	135.00
Row 6, 2.	HATPIN, *Art Nouveau*, French Ivory w/marbleized insert, 2¾" head. Circa: 1910	65.00
Row 6, 3.	HATPIN, Imitation ivory celluloid 1¾" scallop shell, *Art Deco* design, a symbol for safe travel. Circa: 1920	35.00
Row 6, 4.	HATPIN, Hand-painted, patterned plastic, *Art Deco*. 2¾" head. Circa: 1920	55.00
Row 6, 5.	HATPIN, Full figural celluloid molded 2½" elephant head on 5½" pin. Circa: 1910	95.00
Row 6, 6.	HATPIN, Art Deco, 2¼" pierced or cut two-mold celluloid. Circa: 1920	35.00
Row 6, 7.	HATPIN, Stylized *Art Deco* painted celluloid scallop shell. Circa: 1920	45.00
Row 6, 8.	HAT ORNAMENT, Plastic golf club set w/rhinestones. Circa: 1925	55.00

PLATE 27
From the Collection of: Baker

PLATE 28.

ROW & NO.	DESCRIPTION	VALUE
Row 1, 1.	PENDANT, *Art Deco*, gilt on brass w/Bohemian glass "*Moonstone.*" Circa: 1930	110.00
Row 1, 2.	BEADS, *Art Deco*, w/pendant, Venetian glass w/gilt peirced links, emerald-color rhinestones, barrel clasp. Circa: 1930	135.00
Row 1, 3.	NECKLACE, *Art Nouveau*, w/umber and pink iridescent wax-base pearls. Circa: 1915	85.00
Top Row 1, 4.	BROOCH, *Art Deco*, enamel on brass w/molded Bakelite center. Circa: 1925	65.00
Center Row 1, 5.	BROOCH, Mosaic, set gypsy fashion w/twisted ribbon vermicelli-work on frame. Circa: 1897	75.00
Bottom Row 1, 6.	BROOCH, *Art Deco*, gilt on brass w/imitation stones and Bakelite center set. Circa: 1925	75.00
Top Row 1, 7.	EARRINGS, Brass, Phoenix bird, Egyptian motif w/imitation jade. Circa: 1920	45.00
Bottom Row 1, 8.	PENDANT, Enamel and silver w/gold wash, "Good Luck" symbol, Chinese. Circa: 1900	65.00
Row 1, 9.	NECKLACE, Victorian, gilt on brass set w/*baroque* Persian pearls and French Jet. Circa: 1897	135.00
Top Row 2, 1.	SCENT BOTTLE & LORGNETTE, Elephant hair, man's monocle chain shown w/pressed glass scent bottle. Chain, Circa: 1870. Bottle Circa:1900	Chain 145.00 Bottle 85.00
Center Row 2, 2.	BRACELET, Gilt engraved links w/3 carnelian carved monkeys and dangling elephant charm. Circa: 1900	110.00
Bottom Row 2, 3.	BRACELET, Gold base metal slide-type bracelet, imitation stones w/unusual snap fastener. Circa: 1925	75.00
Right Row 2, 4.	CAMEO, Shell, white gold filigree w/imitation diamonds, Circa: 1935	75.00
Right Row 2, 5.	BRACELET, Gold w/Persian turquoise and half pearls. Circa: 1895	325.00
Row 3, 1.	WATCH, Man's pocket watch, Bulova, 17 jewel in 14K gold-plated case, "*25 yr. warranty.*" Circa: 1920	450.00
Row 3, 2.	WATCH PIN & LOCKET, Victorian gold-filled pin, green and pink gold w/locket set w/cabochon gartnets and diamond, w/lock of hair inside and name, "*Robert Burke.*" Pin, Circa: 1890. Locket, Circa: 1895	Pin 65.00 Locket 125.00
Row 3, 3.	CUFF LINKS, Rare collector's piece w/photo. Circa: 1910	55.00
Row 3, 4.	PURSE, Sterling and enamel mesh. Circa: 1925	325.00
Row 3, 5.	WATCH CHAIN & FOB, Man's fob and vest chain, gilt over brass wire w/shell, w/mother-of-pearl horse head fob. Circa: 1910	110.00
Row 3, 6.	WATCH, Large, heavy man's watch, 17 jewel, gold-filled, 25 yr. warranty, Hampden Watch Co., Canton, Ohio. Circa: 1888	525.00
Row 3, 7.	CUFF BUTTONS, Man's snap-on, mother-of-pearl in sterling. Circa: 1920	25.00
Row 4, 1.	WATCH, Woman's, Elgin, 14K w/*fleur de lis* watch pin w/chain and onyx button-pin. Circa: 1875	650.00
Row 4, 2.	CUFF LINKS, Man's engraved 10K gold. Circa: 1920	45.00
Row 4, 3.	LOCKET, Exceptionally large gold-filled locket, "S.G. & Co." w/smoke-color rhinestones, obverse side engraved: "*From Alvin.*" Circa: 1915	85.00

PLATE 28

From the Collections of: Vaught • Henning • Warren •
Baker • Ginny's Antiques Et Cetera

PLATE 29.

ROW & NO.	DESCRIPTION	VALUE
Row 1, 1.	BEADS, Amber-color Bohemian glass, single strand. Circa: 1920	75.00
Row 1, 2.	BEADS, Extremely long single-strand crystal and citrine-color Bohemian glass. Circa: 1902	85.00
Row 1, 3.	BEADS, Peking glass, Venetian. Circa: 1930	75.00
Row 1, 4.	BEADS, Venetian art glass type beads w/gold flecks, art glass (Murano, Italy). Circa: 1930	145.00
Row 1, 5.	BELT, Rope of Czech, beads w/tassels (could be used as necklace). Circa: 1920	95.00
Row 2, 1.	BROOCH, Rhodium and enamel, marked "MB". Circa: 1940	65.00
Row 2, 2.	BROOCH, Rhinestone and simulated wax-bead pearls, marked "Regency". Circa: 1930	75.00
Row 2, 3.	BROOCH, Simulated topaz w/tassels. Circa: 1930	45.00
Row 2, 4.	BROOCH, Simulated amethyst and rhinestone. Circa: 1930	55.00
Row 2, 5.	BROOCH, Exceptional workmanship, delicate floral spray pin w/simulated gemstones. Circa: 1930	75.00
Row 3, 1.	BROOCH, Floral w/simulated gemstones. Circa: 1940	45.00
Row 3, 2.	BROOCH, Glass beads and simulated pearls on rhodium. Circa: 1940	35.00
Row 3, 3.	BROOCH, Bohemian glass, marked; "Coro". Circa: 1940	45.00
Row 3, 4.	BROOCH, Gold wash on silver, marked: "Trifari". Circa: 1940	55.00
Row 3, 5.	BROOCH, Varied cuts of simulated gemstones. Circa: 1940	35.00
Row 4, 1.	BROOCH, Gold wash over silver w/metallic corded tassels. Circa: 1910	35.00
Row 4, 2.	SCARF PIN, Exquisitely wrought w/tiny definitive bees on hinged flowers, w/safety nib, signed; "Miriam Haskell". Circa: 1930	185.00
Row 4, 3.	BROOCH, Sterling w/coral and turquoise drops. Circa: 1920	85.00
Row 4, 4.	CROSS W/CHAIN, Woven metallic gold thread chain w/extravagantly decorated gothic cross, simulated gemstones. Circa: 1930	95.00

PLATE 29
From the Collection of: Alexander

PLATE 30.

ROW & NO.	DESCRIPTION	VALUE
Row 1, 1.	VANITY CASE, *Art Deco*, German silver and enamel powder compact. Circa: 1920	250.00
Row 1, 2.	VANITY CASE, *Art Deco*, electroplated nickel silver w/gold wash (EPNS), coin and lipstick case. Circa: 1925	275.00
Row 1, 3.	BROOCH, *Art Moderne* stylized, goldplated, marked: "*Coro.*" Circa: 1940	95.00
Row 2, 1.	NECKLACE, *Art Deco* sterling and enamel w/lapis-color Bohemian glass. Circa: 1925	225.00
Row 2, 2.	NECKLACE, *Art Moderne* Bakelite and celluloid. Circa: 1925	250.00
Row 2, 3.	NECKLACE, *Art Moderne* Bakelite and chrome. Circa: 1930	275.00
Row 2, 4.	NECKLACE, *Art Moderne* Bakelite and chrome. Circa: 1930	275.00
Row 2, 5.	NECKLACE, Gilt, Czechoslavakian lapis-color glass w/exquisite enamel. Circa: 1920	225.00
Row 3, 1.	PENDANT, Brass and Bakelite with woven grosgrain silk, w/brass slide, "Tut's Tomb" motif. Circa: 1925	250.00
Row 3, 2.	WRISTWATCH, *Art Deco*, Elgin, gold filled (working condition). Circa: 1920	550.00
Row 3, 3.	RING, *Art Deco*, pierced shank on either side, enamel and gold. Circa: 1925	185.00
Row 3, 4.	EARRINGS, *Art Deco*, transition to *Moderne*, w/clip backs, enamel and chrome. Circa: 1930	150.00

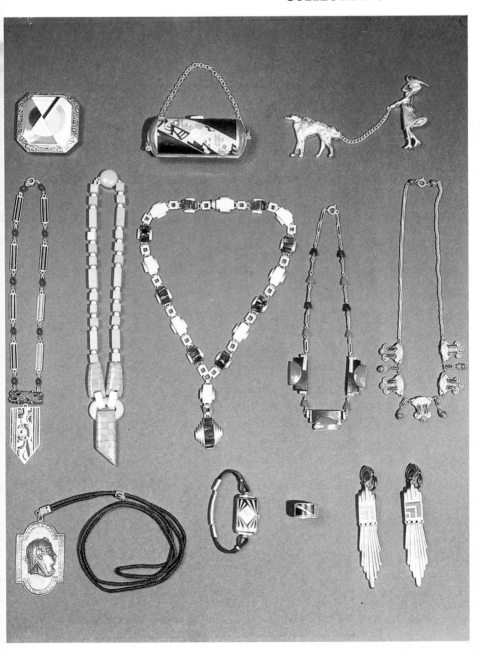

PLATE 30
From the Collection of: Antiques From Alota

PLATE 31.

ROW & NO.	DESCRIPTION	VALUE

Pin Cushion

Top

Row 1, 1. TIE OR CRAVAT PINS, All 14K gold w/precious stones: opals, amethysts, rubies, emeralds, diamonds, pearls. Circa: 1890-1930 — 75.00-250.00

Center

Row 1, 2. CRAVAT PIN, Gold wash over brass, large advertising pin, marked "*John Deere Plough*". Circa: 1870 — 75.00

Bottom

Row 1, 3. BAR PINS, A. Silver color w/rhinestones. Circa: 1930 — 20.00
B. Sterling w/French paste, marked: "ALLCo". Circa: 1910 — 35.00
C. Silver filigree w/imitation sapphires. Circa: 1900 — 50.00
D. Gold w/cabochon opal and pearls. Circa: 1900 — 225.00

Row 2, 1. PERFUME BOTTLE, Venetian ribbon glass, for *chatelaine* w/crystal stopper. Engraved, gold wash on silver (rare). Circa: 1850 — 175.00

Row 2, 2. RING IN BOX, Enamel and porcelain portrait, sterling silver shank. Original box, oriental silk-covered. Circa: 1890 — 225.00

Row 2, 3. BROOCH, Shell cameo, 14K gold, gypsy setting, plain frame. Circa: 1920 — 150.00

Row 2, 4. BRACELET, Shell cameo encased in cuff bracelet, gold wash over silver. Circa: 1900 — 275.00

Row 2, 5. BROOCH, Heavy, gold memorial piece w/marble stone *Pietra Dura* mosaic, set in black marble w/2 locks of hair behind glass in reverse side. Circa: 1850 — 375.00

Row 2, 6. PERFUME, Enameled Venetian glass *chatelaine* w/chain and stopper, hinged cap fastener, gold. Circa: 1850 — 185.00

Row 3, 1. BROOCH, Mourning jet. Circa: 1890 — 45.00

Row 3, 2. EARRINGS, Jet w/wire for pierced ears, teardrop style. Circa: 1900 — 35.00

Row 3, 3. EARRINGS, Jet w/wire for pierced ears, tassel style. Circa: 1890 — 45.00

Row 3, 4. BARRETT, Hair ornament, jet glass, cut and faceted French Jet. Circa: 1890 — 35.00

Row 4, 1. *CHATELAINE*, Spectacles case, hallmarked sterling, Birmingham, England (sterling rim spectacles, 1890). Case, Circa: 1905 — Case only 285.00

Row 4, 2. SCENT BOTTLE, Finger ring and palm-size scent bottle, sterling hallmarked, enamel thistles, English. Circa: 1898 — 150.00

Row 4, 3. PERFUME, German silver, unmarked, palm-size, missing chain. Circa: 1900 — 65.00

Row 4, 4. *VINAIGERETTE*, German silver, unmarked, heart-shape, for *chatelaine*. Circa: 1900 — 125.00

Row 4, 5. PERFUME, Mother-of-pearl, palm-size with finger ring, gold Circa: 1890 — 125.00

Row 4, 6. BOUQUET HOLDER, (Bridal) silver *baroque*, w/handkerchief ring, belt or bosom clip. Circa: 1850 — 275.00

Row 4, 7. BOUQUET HOLDER, (Bridal) silver, *baroque*, missing chain w/ring. Circa: 1895 — 275.00

Row 4, 8. BOUQUET HOLDER, (Bridal) bronze and silver w/bronze wire filigree, *Art Nouveau* w/belt or bosom clip. Circa: 1895 — 350.00

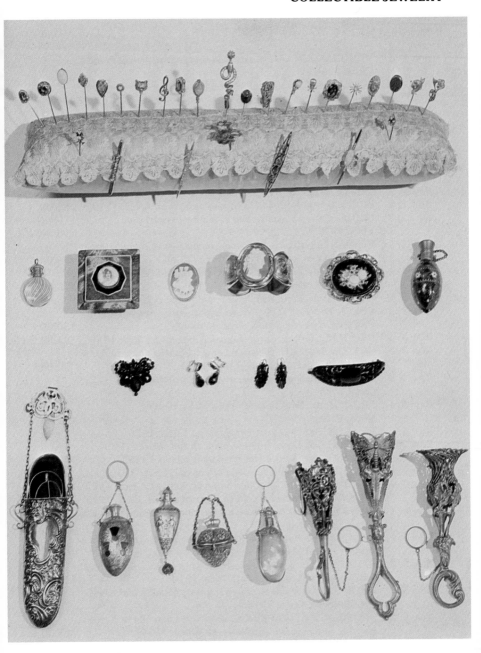

PLATE 31
From the Collection of: Alexander

PLATE 32.

ROW & NO.	DESCRIPTION	VALUE
Row 1, 1.	MEMORANDUM BOOK, *Art Nouveau*, silver/pencil (French). Circa: 1890	100.00
Row 1, 2.	MATCH SAFE, w/striker, *Art Nouveau*, silver (Birmingham, England). Circa: 1901	135.00
Row 1, 3.	MATCH SAFE, w/striker, *Art Nouveau*, 800 silver, Circa: 1900	110.00
Row 1, 4.	MATCH SAFE, w/striker, *Art Nouveau*, silver (American), Unger Bros., Newark, N.J. Circa: 1900	250.00
Row 1, 5.	CIGARETTE CASE, *Art Nouveau*, silver w/gold wash Circa: 1910	325.00
Row 2, 1.	VANITY CASE, *Art Deco*, silver mesh w/enamel. Circa: 1925	175.00
Row 2, 2.	BROOCH, *Art Nouveau* in copper and silver. Circa: 1910	85.00
Row 2, 3.	BROOCH, *Art Nouveau*, silver w/mother-of-pearl inlay Circa: 1910	95.00
Row 2, 4.	PENDANT, *Art Deco*, (obverse) summer/youth, and (reverse) winter/old age, sterling (rare). Circa: 1920	175.00
Row 3, 1.	BROOCH, *Art Nouveau*, sterling (925), Unger Bros., Newark, N.J. Circa: 1900	175.00
Row 3, 2.	BROOCH, *Art Nouveau*, base metal. Circa: 1902	35.00
Row 3, 3.	CHECK WARRANTOR, *Art Nouveau*, purse-size, Unger Bros., *Pat. Jan. 7, 1902* (rare). Circa: 1902	150.00
Row 3, 4.	BROOCH, Sterling, *Jorge Jensen* (Denmark). Circa: 1930	95.00
Row 3, 5.	BUTTON-BROOCH, Silver and enamel button converted into brooch, marked "Alpacca". Circa: 1900	35.00
Row 3, 6.	BROOCH, Sterling, *Jorge Jenson*, *Art Deco* (Denmark). Circa: 1925	85.00
Row 4, 1.	BROOCH, *Art Nouveau*, (900) silver w/lapis stone. Circa: 1910	125.00
Row 4, 2.	BROOCH, *Art Deco*, set/chrysoprase. Circa: 1920	85.00
Row 4, 3.	BROOCH, *Art Deco*, brass w/glass stones. Circa: 1920	55.00
Row 4, 4.	BROOCH, *Art Deco*, silver w/enamel. Circa: 1915	45.00
Row 4, 5.	BROOCH, *Art Nouveau*, silver w/enamel. Circa: 1910	65.00
Row 4, 6.	BROOCH, Stylized *Art Deco* butterfly, enamel. Circa: 1920	125.00
Row 4, 7.	BROOCH, *Art Nouveau*, gold and enamel w/opal. Circa: 1910	145.00
Row 5, 1.	BUCKLE/PIN, *Art Nouveau*, buckle converted into a brooch, Unger Bros. Circa: 1900	175.00
Row 5, 2.	BROOCH, *Art Nouveau* dragonfly, base metal, colored glass stone. Circa: 1910	65.00
Row 5, 3.	CAPE BUCKLE, 2 pc., marked; "*Copper-Doré*", bronze finish, (attributed to Tiffany Studio). Circa: 1910	110.00
Row 6, 1.	DRESS CLIPS, 1 pair w/patent imprint, Bakelite and metal, *Art Moderne*. Circa: 1925	95.00
Row 6, 2.	SET: BRACELET, EARRINGS, Screw-type and clip bracelet, Bakelite and chrome, *Art Moderne*. Circa: 1930	275.00
Row 6, 3.	BROOCH, *Art Nouveau*, Sterling set w/hematite stone. Circa: 1910	125.00

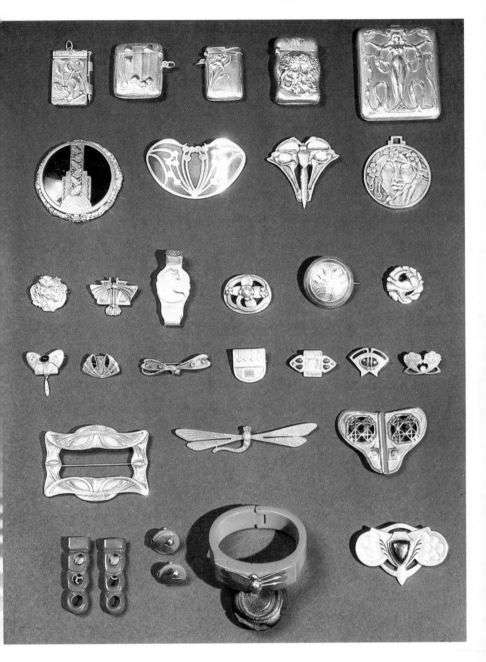

PLATE 32
From the Collection of: Antiques From Alota

PLATE 33.

ROW & NO.	DESCRIPTION	VALUE
Row 1, 1.	WATCH, Woman's gold engraved Hamilton case for watch (no movement--used as locket). Circa: 1910	85.00
Row 1, 2.	BROOCH, *Plique'A Jour* enamel, w/smoke-color paste stones. Circa: 1940	95.00
Row 1, 3.	WATCH, Woman's Elgin, gold watch ornately engraved. Circa: 1881	650.00
Row 1, 4.	BROOCH, Hand-painted porcelain, Limoges, France, in gold frame. Circa: 1900	135.00
Row 1, 5.	BROOCH, Shell cameo in filigree frame (see Plate 5 for detailed photograph). Circa: 1895	135.00
Row 1, 6.	BROOCH, Synthetic cameo in silver mounting and synthetic diamond. Circa: 1930	45.00
Row 1, 7.	BROOCH, Shell cameo in gold frame (damaged shell). Circa: 1900	100.00
Row 2, 1.	BROOCH, Portrait in heavy *baroque* gilt frame. Circa: 1900	85.00
Row 2, 2.	WATCH, Man's, Tavannes Watch Co., engraved gold, 17 jewel Swiss, warranted 25 years. Circa: 1910	325.00
Row 2, 3.	BROOCH, Hand-painted portrait in silver frame. Circa: 1925	75.00
Row 2, 4.	BROOCH, Coin, cut-out, silver (Coin of Realm). Circa: 1920	35.00
Row 2, 5.	BROOCH, Wax-bead pearls. Circa: 1910	25.00
Row 2, 6.	BROOCH, Wax-bead pearls. Circa:1930	10.00
Row 2, 7.	BROOCH, Sterling w/French paste stones. Circa: 1950	35.00
Row 3, 1.	NECKLACE, Reproduction in gold wash metal and synthetic coral of Victorian piece. Circa: 1930	85.00
Row 3, 2.	LOCKET, Gold wash w/chain fashioned of pure gold nuggets. Circa: 1910	850.00
Row 3, 3.	PENDANT, Amber w/insect embedded in natural element on 14K chain. Circa: 1925	225.00
	With Chain	285.00
Row 3, 4.	NECKLACE, Marked silver w/turquoise, American Indian design. Circa: 1940	325.00
Row 3, 5.	BROOCH, Lapel pin w/imitation turquoise. Indian reproduction. Circa: 1920	45.00
Row 3, 6.	NECKLACE, German-cut crystal w/Peking glass pendant set w/filigree white gold and pearls. Circa: 1930	250.00
Row 4, 1.	EARRINGS, Victorian, gold w/old-style plunger-stud wires. Circa: 1860	95.00
Row 4, 2.	BROOCH, Flower or corsage pin, gold w/turquoise and pearl. Circa: 1860	125.00
Row 4, 3.	CAPE OR JERSEY PINS, w/chain, gold. Circa: 1850	75.00
Row 4, 4.	HAIR ORNAMENT, Ivory and jet on brass pin, Circa: 1890	45.00
Row 4, 5.	BROOCH, Mosaic (Italy). Circa: 1910	35.00
Row 4, 6.	WATCH, Woman's wristwatch, Emerson, set w/paste stones. Circa: 1930	275.00
Row 4, 7.	BROOCH, 18K gold set w/cabochon-cut coral. Circa: 1925	110.00
Row 4, 8.	HAIR CLIPS, Pr. of decorative "Bobby" pins, set w/rhinestones. Circa: 1940	25.00
Row 4, 9.	HAIR PIN, Decorative hair pin w/gilt filigree and wax-bead pearls. Circa: 1930	10.00
Row 4, 10.	STUDS, Woman's, hand-painted porcelain blouse studs, Limoges, France. Circa: 1890	125.00

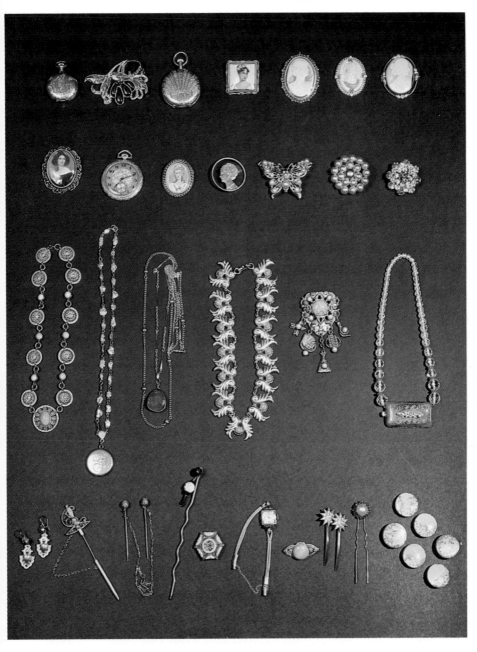

PLATE 33

From the Collections of: Baker • Barlow • Nance •
Ginny's Antiques, Et Cetera • Anonymous

PLATE 34.

ROW & NO.	DESCRIPTION	VALUE
Row 1, 1.	SASH BUCKLE, Sterling silver. Circa: 1920	65.00
Row 1, 2.	HAT BUCKLE, Sterling filigree w/ French Jet, used as accent for *Aigrette*. Circa: 1900	65.00
Row 1, 3.	BUCKLE FOR RIBBON OR SASH, Cut and polished steel beads. Circa: 1870	55.00
Row 1, 4.	BELT BUCKLE, Sterling silver, large, *baroque*. Circa: 1900	75.00
Row 2, 1.	BELT BUCKLE, Rhinestone w/brass hasp. Circa: 1930	35.00
Row 2, 2.	BROOCH, Sterling silver w/simulated hasp. Circa: 1910	55.00
Row 2, 3.	BELT BUCKLE, Double hasp, made of Egyptian-vintage (Arabic year) 1293 coins (King Farouk). Circa: 1910	85.00
Row 2, 4.	HAT BUCKLE, Silver openwork. Circa: 1910	35.00
Row 2, 5.	CAPE BUCKLE, *Art Nouveau*, sterling and jet (½ unit). Circa: 1900	45.00
Row 3, 1.	BUCKLE, *Art Nouveau*, gold wash over sterling w/simulated amethyst. Circa: 1900	75.00
Row 3, 2.	SASH BUCKLE, *Art Nouveau*, bezel-set simulated amethyst, gold wash over sterling. Circa: 1900	125.00
Row 3, 3.	BELT BUCKLE, *Art Deco*, double hasp, gold wash. Circa: 1920	85.00
Row 3, 4.	SASH BUCKLE, *Art Nouveau*, gold wash over silver. Circa: 1900	85.00
Row 4, 1.	SET: SASH ORNAMENT & BELT BUCKLES, *Art Nouveau*, sash ornament, sterling w/matching buckles for belt or cape. Circa: 1910	285.00
Row 5, 1.	BUCKLES, *Art Deco*, belt or coat buckles, silver. Circa: 1920	45.00
Row 5, 2.	BUCKLE, ½ pair *Art Nouveau cloisonne* belt or cape buckle (to show workmanship). Circa: 1910	NP
Row 5, 3.	BUCKLE, Filigree silver, cape or belt. Circa: 1920	35.00
Row 5, 4.	BUCKLE, Exquisite *cloisonne* belt or cape buckles (rare). Circa: 1897	250.00
Row 6, 1.	BELT BUCKLE, Mother-of-pearl w/chrome hasp. Circa: 1930	25.00
Row 6, 2.	BUCKLE, Ornamental slide for belt or hat, sterling and enamel, *Art Deco*. Circa: 1920	25.00
Row 6, 3.	BELT BUCKLE, Mother-of-Pearl w/chrome hasp. Circa: 1930	25.00
Row 7, 1.	BELT BUCKLE, Gold wash over silver w/cabochon-cut amethysts for eyes and accents (rare). Circa: 1920	325.00

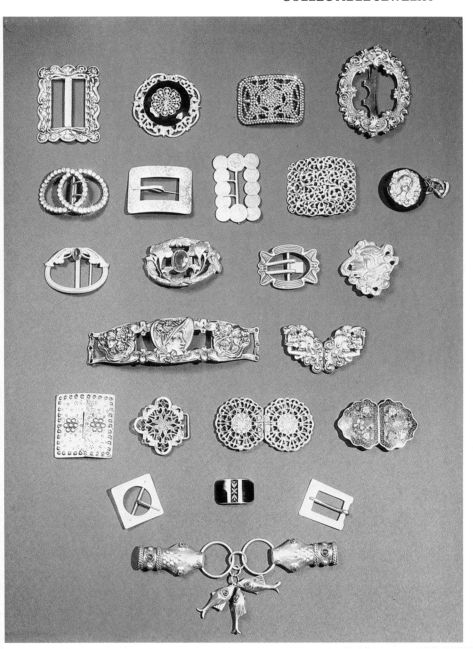

PLATE 34

From the Collection of: Alexander

PLATE 35.

ROW & NO.	DESCRIPTION	VALUE
Row 1, 1.	BROOCH, Marked: "sterling" and *"Danecraft,"* very heavy silver, 4½" beak to tail feathers. Circa: 1940	125.00
Row 1, 2.	MEMO CASE, (Replacement pencil) silver-color *Art Nouveau, Repoussé.* Reverse: Festival Hall & Cascades, *"World's Fair, St. Louis 1904."* Circa: 1904	85.00
Row 1, 3.	LAPEL PIN, Sterling reproduction of 17th Century pendants. Circa: 1930	35.00
Row 1, 4.	HAIR ORNAMENT, Sterling filigree on double-prong hair pin w/trembler spring. Circa: 1870	65.00
Row 1, 5.	BROOCH, Sterling w/amethyst-cut stones depicting blossoms. Circa: 1940	125.00
Row 2, 1.	BROOCH, Sterling, floral. Circa: 1930	35.00
Row 2, 2.	SET: NECKLACE, EARRINGS, *Art Moderne,* rhodium or chrome finish, exceptionally fine chain. Circa: 1935	125.00
Row 2, 3.	BROOCH, Sterling w/onyx setting in shield. Circa: 1940	85.00
Row 2, 4.	SET: NECKLACE, EARRINGS, Gold wash chain and tassels, beautiful chain work. Circa: 1935	85.00
Row 3, 1.	CUMBERBUND BUCKLE, Belt or sash buckle, loops on reverse side, one-piece design, oxidized silver. Circa: 1925	55.00
Row 3, 2.	BROOCH, Oxidized filigree silver w/synthetic turquoise stones. Circa: 1930	20.00
Row 4, 1.	BRACELET, Sterling and jet bangle. Circa: 1900	110.00
Row 4, 2.	BROOCH, French Jet wired on japanned metal, (reproduction of 1860 pin). Circa: 1950	45.00
Row 4, 3.	ROPE NECKLACE OR BELT, Fine crochet, French Jet Bohemian beads. Circa: 1920	110.00
Row 4, 4.	EARRINGS, Jet glass and rhinestones, screw-type. Circa: 1930	25.00
Row 4, 5.	EARRINGS, Faceted jet, screw-type. Circa: 1930	20.00
Row 4, 6.	BEADS, Ebony wood beads, to resemble true jet. Circa: 1925	35.00

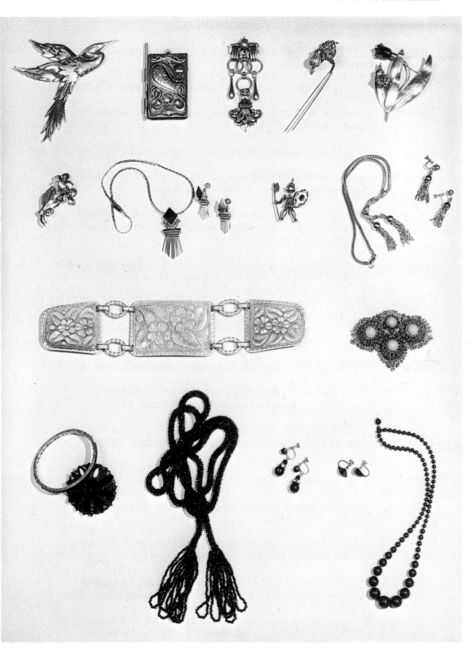

PLATE 35

From the Collections of: Baker • Nance • Marshall •
    Ginny's Antiques, Et Cetera

PLATE 36.

ROW & NO.	DESCRIPTION	VALUE
Row 1, 1.	LAVALIERE, 18K gold pendant, 14K chain, delicate workmanship (slightly damaged). Circa: 1850	150.00
Row 1, 2.	LAVALIERE, Silver filigree, paste crystal-color stones w/jet. Circa: 1900	45.00
Row 1, 3.	LAVALIERE, Gold wash, filigree pendant w/enamel and wax-bead pearls. Circa: 1910	45.00
Row 1, 4.	LAVALIERE, 14K gold rings and chain set w/half pearls. Circa: 1925	125.00
Row 1, 5.	LAVALIERE, Gold wash over silver w/stone cameo, 2 imitation sapphires, and Venetian beads. Circa: 1910	65.00
Row 1, 6.	LOCKET OR FOB, Engraved gold, contains 2 photographs, worn as locket but originally watch fob. (Chain for display only. Priced on Plate 41.) Circa: 1915	85.00
Row 2, 1.	NECKLACE, Art Deco, gilt on brass, engraved, Egyptian motif w/blown iridescent glass drops and cobalt blue beads. Circa: 1925	650.00
Row 3, 1.	BEADS, Bohemian imitation garnet beads. Circa: 1930	55.00
Row 3, 2.	BEADS, Crochet, finely-cut and faceted Bohemian beads, long rope. Circa: 1930	125.00
Row 3, 3.	NECKLACE, Gilt and enamel w/Venetian red glass beads. Circa: 1920	85.00
Row 3, 4.	BEADS, Hand-made necklace of beads and shells sold at Inwood, N.Y., Indian reservation. (Rare). Circa: 1927	25.00
Row 4, 1.	GLOVE HOLDER, Gold mesh w/clasp and tassel and finger ring. May be used for fan or handkerchief. Circa: 1890	65.00
Row 4, 2.	PENDANT, Child's shell cameo, set in gilt engraved frame, w/loop for chain. Circa: 1915	25.00
Row 4, 3.	BAR PIN, Wedgwood blue and white jasper, set in engraved sterling. Circa: 1875	65.00
Row 4, 4.	EARRINGS, Imitation garnet in 10K gold, w/wires set w/one garnet each. Circa: 1930	35.00
Row 4, 5.	BROOCH, Branch coral set in 14K gold wire mount. (Advertised in Harper's Bazaar, (Nov, 1910), Baird-North Co., Providence, R.I.). Circa: 1910	45.00
Row 4, 6.	BRACELET, Mesh gilt w/mother-of pearl in buckle fastener. Circa: 1910	65.00

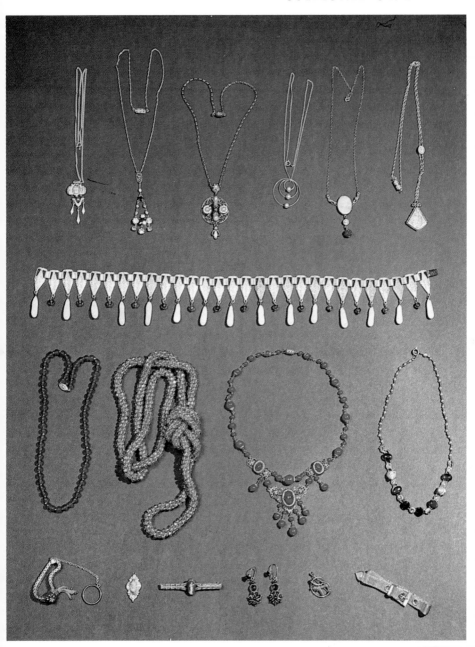

PLATE 36
From the Collections of: Baker • Mills

PLATE 37.

ROW & NO.	DESCRIPTION	VALUE
Row 1, 1.	NECKLACE, Damescene, *Art Nouveau.* Circa: 1910	125.00
Row 2, 1.	BROOCH, Sterling silver filigree. Circa: 1940	45.00
Row 2, 2.	BROOCH, Gold wash over sterling, simulated turquoise and lapis. Circa: 1950	85.00
Row 2, 3.	BROOCH, Seed pearl spray on gold wash wire. Circa: 1920	85.00
Row 2, 4.	BROOCH, Sterling filigree cage, bee set w/gemstone; floral w/imitation coral. Circa: 1940	85.00
Row 3, 1.	BROOCH, Half pearls in gold set w/center rose-cut diamond. Circa: 1900	150.00
Row 3, 2.	BROOCH, Sterling, engraved, *repoussé.* Circa: 1930	45.00 pr.
Row 3, 3.	PINS, Pair of sterling, engraved, *repoussé.* Circa: 1930	55.00
Row 3, 4.	BROOCH, "Paperweight" pin, gold wash, gypsy set, gold bead frame. Circa: 1895	45.00
Row 3, 5.	WATCH PIN, Gold wash over sterling, imitation pearls in leaf design. Circa: 1895	75.00
Row 4, 1.	BRACELET, Filigree gold wash over silver, set w/genuine cabochon-cut amethysts. Circa: 1940	250.00
Row 5, 1.	BROOCH, Enamel on sterling, butterfly. Circa: 1900	35.00
Row 5, 2.	BROOCH, Enamel on sterling, owls w/marcasites. Circa: 1900	75.00
Row 5, 3.	BROOCH, Enamel on sterling, frog, child's pin. Circa: 1900	75.00
Row 5, 4.	BROOCH, Sterling, heavy, initial pin. Circa: 1900	25.00
Row 5, 5.	BROOCH, French enamel, Siamese cat. Circa: 1900	85.00
Row 5, 6.	BROOCH, French enamel, rooster w/marcasites. Circa: 1900	110.00
Row 6, 1.	*LAVALIERE, Art Nouveau* gold w/amethyst and seed pearls, w/baroque pearl drop. Circa: 1900	325.00
Row 6, 2.	EARRINGS, Faceted crystal, (colorless quartz), gold wire. Circa: 1895	65.00
Row 6, 3.	EARRINGS, Faceted crystal, (colorless quartz), screw-back. Circa: 1920	55.00
Row 6, 4	EARRINGS & BAR PIN SET, Pierced and engraved gold w/half pearls, w/matching earrings on wire. Circa: 1860	175.00
Row 7, 1.	EARRINGS, BRACELET, BROOCH, *PARURE,* Gold wash on sterling, enameled w/metal tag "*Denmark.*" Circa: 1950	150.00
Row 8, 1.	PENDANT, Gold wash pendant w/heavy chain, pendant set w/simulated moonstones and garnets w/gold-color rope tassel. Circa: 1920	85.00

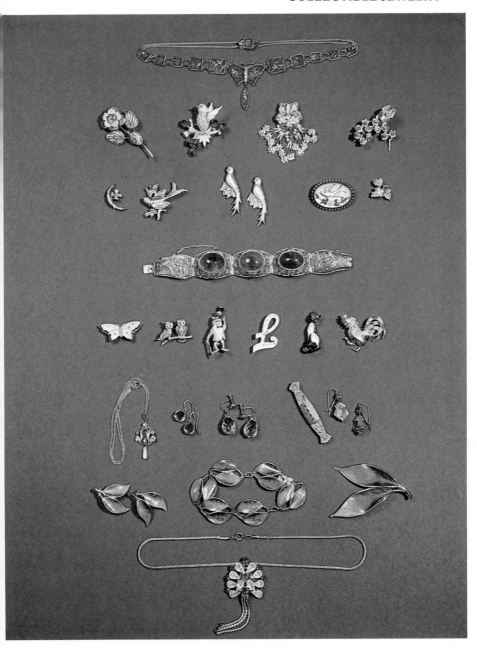

PLATE 37

From the Collection of: Alexander

PLATE 38.

ROW & NO.	DESCRIPTION	VALUE
Row 1, 1.	BROOCH, Wedgwood jasperware, vertical oval, brooch/pendant w/gold chain, twisted gold frame, seed pearls, classical figure w/urn. Circa: 1875	325.00
Row 2, 1.	BROOCH, Wedgwood jasperware, 14K yellow gold frame w/seed pearls, Hackwood cupids. (William Hackwood modeled from 1769-1832). Circa: 1860	275.00
Row 2, 2.	BROOCH, Wedgwood jasperware, horizontal oval, brooch/pendant, sterling mounting, Hackwood's "*Cupids at Play*". Circa: 1890	225.00
Row 3, 1.	BROOCH, Wedgwood jasperware, sterling frame, *Melpomene*, "The Singer", one of the Nine Muses. She is portrayed w/tragic mask and club of Hercules. (Modeled 1777 by John Flaxman). Circa: 1880	195.00
Row 3, 2.	PERFUME FLASK, Wedgwood jasperware, flask, purse size 4½". The beautiful-voiced muse, *Calliope*, w/roll of music paper. *Reverse*: The muse, *Euterpe*, (also called *Tibana*), who presided over lyric poetry w/flute or *tibiae* pipes. Circa: 1910	275.00
Row 4, 1.	VANITY CASE, Wedgwood jasperware, sterling compact for loose powder, by Stratton of England, still being produced, *"Three Graces"* or *Charities* of Greek mythology: *Aglaia* (the radiant), *Thalia* (the flowering), *Euphrosyne* (joy); companions of Venus, who endowed beauty, charm, and wisdom on mortals. Circa: 1950	285.00

PLATE 38
From the Collection of: Mills

PLATE 39.

                     DESCRIPTION   VALUE

Top Left

1.   JEWEL BOX, Bronze, *Art Nouveau*, satin lining, marked
"*DEPOSE*" (French). Circa: 1890   150.00

2.   CAMEO, Onyx, w/chain, in 10K Roman and rose gold.
Circa: 1880   135.00

3.   SEVEN PENDANTS,

L-R   14 K, seed pearls, sapphire and diamond, Circa: 1910   165.00

Victorian cameo w/fresh-water pearls w/chain. Circa: 1895   185.00

Oriental jade angel fish w/modern 14K gold chain. Circa: 1925   135.00

w/Baroque pearl and seed pearl drops. Circa: 1900   150.00

Jade and coral w/fine link chain. Circa: 1910   135.00

Gold w/opal and *baroque* fresh-water pearl. Circa: 1910   150.00

Gold w/two rubies. Circa: 1910   135.00

Top Center
L-R

1.   BROOCH, Marcasites and carnelian set in sterling. Circa: 1920   110.00

2.   EARRINGS, Marcasites in sterling w/carnelian bead drops,
Circa: 1920   95.00

3.   CLIP, Marcasite and sterling shoe or dress clip. Circa: 1930   45.00

Top Right
L-R   SIX RINGS,

1.   Marcasite and sterling. Circa: 1920   85.00

2.   Marcasite and onyx, set in sterling. Circa: 1930   85.00

3.   Marcasite in sterling. Circa: 1930   75.00

4.   Sterling and marcasite. Circa: 1920   95.00

5.   Marcasite and jade in sterling. Circa: 1920   85.00

6.   Marcasite and onyx in sterling. Circa: 1920   85.00

Row 2, 1.   EARRINGS, Marcasite in sterling. Circa: 1920   55.00

Top
Row 2, 2.   BRACELET, *Art Deco*, link design, sterling w/marcasites.
Circa: 1925   110.00

Bottom
Row 2, 3.   BROOCH, 14K, white and pink gold, Cartier-designed rabbit
w/*baroque* pearl head, ruby eyes, and turquoise stones.
Circa: 1935   375.00

Row 3, 1.   PENDANT-NECKLACE, *Art Nouveau*, set w/tiny opal and
ruby. Circa: 1900   150.00

Row 3, 2.   10 RINGS

1. (L-R)   14K white gold w/emerald and diamonds. Circa: 1920   350.00

14K gold w/cabochon and rose cut garnets. Circa: 1900   300.00

14K gold, onyx set w/diamond. Circa: 1910   250.00

ROW & NO.	DESCRIPTION	VALUE
2. (L-R)	14K gold man's initial birth ring w/diamond and high embossed stork and baby motif. Circa: 1900	250.00
	Platinum, filigree w/diamond. Circa: 1900	950.00
	Platinum, diamonds and sapphires. Circa: 1900	1,100.00
	14K gold, man's wedding or friendship ring, clasped moveable hands, marked: "*Pat. Pending*", w/aquamarine set into palm of hand. Circa: 1890	285.00
3. (L-R)	10K shell cameo, floral motif, set w/diamond. Circa: 1900	175.00
	14K gold, amethyst and pearls w/detailed enameled shank. Circa: 1920	375.00
	Sterling, friendship ring, clasped hands. Circa: 1890	85.00
Row 3, 3.	NECKLACE, Victorian, w/amethyst teardrop stones. Circa: 1900	285.00
Row 4, 1.	FOB, 14K gold w/chrysoprase stone. Circa: 1895	125.00
Row 4, 2.	FOB, "*Knights of Columbus*", gold, helmet lifts; *reverse*, enameled, set w/ruby. Circa: 1910	125.00
Row 4, 3.	CIGAR CUTTER, 14K gold, French, used by actor Charles Laughton in "*Witness for the Prosecution*", marked: "*Pat. Cloi*". Circa: 1940	225.00
Row 4, 4.	FOB STAMP HOLDER, Marked sterling w/Masonic emblem, manufactured by B.M. Co. Circa: 1930	55.00
Row 4, 5.	BRACELET, Victorian, gold wash, set w/six amethysts. Circa: 1890	125.00
Row 4, 6.	BRACELET, 14K gold, child's, engraved. 4¼" round w/original box, velvet lined w/hinge and clasp. Circa: 1890	85.00
Row 4, 7.	5 RINGS, 14K, child's, engraved w/amethysts. Circa: 1910 ea.	55.00
	14K, child's engraved w/heart motif. Circa: 1910	55.00
	10K, infant's, engraved w/scrolls, Circa: 1910	25.00
	14K, twins, engraved matching pair w/set of initials. Circa: 1925 each	55.00
Row 4, 8.	7 HEART LOCKETS,	
	9K back and front, infants's, on chain. Circa: 1930	35.00
	Low karat gold, child's, on chain. Circa: 1935	30.00
	Victorian, 10K, highly engraved and embossed. Circa: 1900	75.00
	Hollow gold set w/small diamond. Circa: 1930	35.00
	3 tiny gold, infant's, one w/small pearl, one hinged as pair. Circa: 1925 each	25.00
Row 5, 1.	BROOCH, Small decorative collar pin, set w/amethysts and half pearls. Circa: 1910	85.00
Row 5, 2.	BREAST PIN, 14K gold, set w/ruby and pearls. Circa: 1910	150.00
Row 5, 3.	BROOCH, Tortoise shell, *pique'* work set w/paste stones. Circa: 1925	150.00

ROW & NO.	DESCRIPTION	VALUE
Row 5, 5.	PENDANT, w/chain, 14K white gold w/2 diamonds and 1 sapphire. Circa: 1925	285.00
Row 5, 6.	LORGNETTE, Silver, folding, w/chain. Circa: 1915	150.00
Row 6, 1.	FOB, Art Nouveau, gold wash, opens w/lock of hair inside under glass. Circa: 1898	110.00
Row 6, 2.	CHARM, 14K gold violin case, set w/rubies and emeralds, w/removable violin; bow, open-lid resin case. Circa: 1930	375.00
Row 6, 3.	EARRINGS, Victorian, 14K gold, filigree w/seed pearl drops. Circa: 1885	150.00
Row 6, 4.	BROOCH, Victorian, 14K gold, sunburst, w/pearls. Circa: 1890	165.00
Row 6, 5.	CAMEO, 14K gold frame, engraved, carved coral, gypsy mounting. Circa: 1900	135.00
Row 6, 6.	BREAST PIN, Low karat gold set w/Bohemian garnets. Circa: 1920	85.00
Row 6, 7.	EARRINGS, Victorian, 14K gold, pendants set w/coral beads in Etruscan-type work. Circa: 1880	165.00
Row 6, 8.	WATCH, Woman's, 18K Roman gold, Elgin, key wind, key set. Circa: 1881	650.00
Row 6, 9.	WATCH, Rolled gold, engraved w/monogram. Circa: 1910	185.00
Row 7, 1.	FOB, 2 watch fobs of human hair, Roman gold jewelers' findings. Circa: 1895	ea. 95.00
Row 7, 2.	WATCH, Presentation, 14K solid gold, Howard Watch Co., very heavy, initials C.P.P. Circa: 1906	2,800.00
Row 7, 3.	WATCH, Howard Watch Co., gold filled and engraved, mass production, note setting screw is at three o'clock; (reproduction are also at three o'clock). Circa: 1900	385.00
Row 7, 4.	WATCH, 14K solid gold, Hamilton, presentation watch, only 2000 made for Dudley, w/all Masonic tools* in 14K gold: "The work of a true and loyal Mason to wear the *square and act upon it in all his daily deeds; to meet all men upon the *level and judge them in accordance with the *compass of truth and charity." (Creed). Circa: 1923	6,500.00

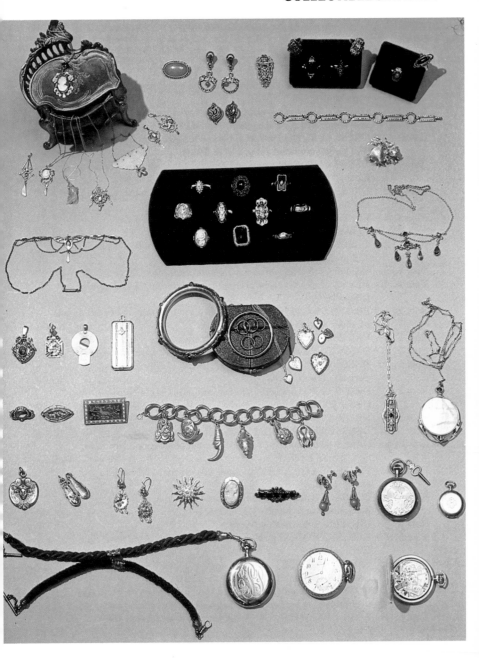

Plate 39

From the Collections of: Biddle • Henning • McCurdy •
Baker • Whittier • Harrison

PLATE 40.

ROW & NO.	DESCRIPTION	VALUE
Row 1, 1.	DRESS CLIP, Oxidized metal set w/varied-color glass beads. Circa: 1930	20.00
Row 1, 2.	DRESS CLIP, Oxidized metal set w/molded glass and rhinestones. Circa: 1930	20.00
Row 1, 3.	DRESS CLIP, Gold wash filigree set w/simulated amethyst and simulated rose zircons. Circa: 1930	20.00
Row 1, 4.	DRESS CLIP, Gold wash and enamel set w/simulated pearls and large simulated ruby. Circa: 1930	20.00
Row 1, 5.	DRESS CLIP, Gold wash and enamel set w/simulated pearls. Circa: 1930	25.00
Row 1, 6.	DRESS CLIP, Etruscan-type metal work, gold wash w/simulated stones. Circa: 1930	20.00
Row 2, 1.	PR. SHOE CLIPS, Finely-cut rhinestones in rhodium. Circa: 1940	pr. 35.00
Row 2, 2.	DRESS CLIP, Very large *Art Deco* style w/simulated pearls and stones. Circa: 1930	75.00
Row 2, 3.	DRESS CLIP, Rhinestones w/simulated topaz. Circa: 1930	20.00
Row 2, 4.	DRESS CLIP, *Art Deco* w/simulated diamonds and sapphire. Circa: 1930	55.00
Row 2, 5.	PR. DRESS CLIPS, *Art Deco* , gold wash w/unusual combination of silver metallic beads. Circa: 1925	pr. 45.00
Row 2, 6.	DRESS CLIP, Cut and faceted fine paste stones. Circa: 1930	25.00
Row 2, 7.	DRESS CLIP, Oxidized metal, die-stamped, gold wash. Circa: 1930	15.00
Row 3, 1.	DRESS CLIP, Oxidized metal w/simulated cabochon-cut garnets. Circa: 1930	25.00
Row 3, 2.	DRESS CLIP, Oxidized metal w/simulated lapis stones. Circa: 1930	20.00
Row 3, 3.	DRESS CLIP, *Art Moderne*, chrome, Circa: 1935	35.00
Row 3, 4.	DRESS CLIP, Wax-bead pearls set in gilt cups Circa: 1930	15.00
Row 3, 5.	DRESS CLIP, Oxidized metal w/unusual treatment for dress clip. Circa: 1925	20.00
Row 3, 6.	PR. SHOE CLIPS, Oxidized and filigree metallic work. Circa: 1940	pr. 35.00
Row 4, 1.	BEADS, Gilt filigree, tubular connectors, cut and faceted Bohemian glass beads. Circa: 1925	75.00
Row 5, 1.	CHOKER, Gilt, mesh w/tassels. Circa: 1940	75.00
Row 6, 1.	DRESS CLIP, Gold wash and enamel, typical *Art Deco*. Circa: 1925	25.00
Row 6, 2.	SASH ORNAMENT, *Art Nouveau*, oxidized brass w/simulated hasp, set w/simulated jade. Circa: 1910	85.00
Row 6, 3.	NECKLACE, Exquisitely cut and individually set paste stones in rhodium, reproduction of heirloom piece. Circa: 1950	135.00
Row 6, 4.	SASH ORNAMENT, Gilt *Art Nouveau* w/simulated ruby. Circa: 1910	45.00
Row 6, 5.	DRESS CLIP, Simulated aquamarines set in white metal Circa: 1935	20.00

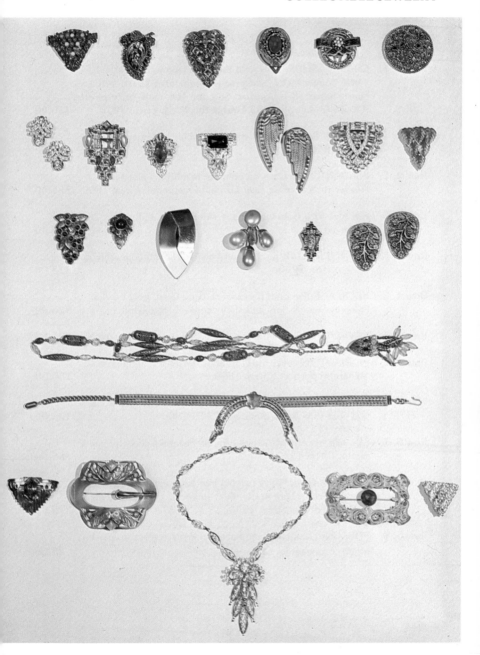

PLATE 40
From the Collection of: Baker

PLATE 41.

ROW & NO.	DESCRIPTION	VALUE
Row 1, 1.	CHAIN W/SLIDE, 14K gold flat link chain w/tab marked "*14K Cowen 1912.*" Reverse insignia dated 1910. 14K heart-shaped slide. Approx. 68", for fan, muff, or *lorgnette*. (Cowen & Malawista, 33 Eldrige St., N.Y.). Circa: 1910	750.00
Row 2, 1.	BAR PIN, Textured gold w/center rubies and diamonds. Circa: 1860	185.00
Row 2, 2.	PENDANT, Gold wash on sterling, beautifully enameled, reverse is clear glass case for photo memorial. Circa: 1860	225.00
Row 2, 3.	BREAST PIN, Gold w/pearls w/safety chain and pin. Circa: 1870	150.00
Row 3, 1.	*LAVALIERE*, 14K gold w/coral cameo, *baroque* pearl w/gold chain. Circa: 1900	375.00
Row 3, 2.	NECKLACE, Pendant necklace w/coral bead, gold beaded links, baroque pearls and shell cameo. Circa: 1850	925.00
Row 3, 3.	*LAVALIERE*, Gold starburst set w/half pearls. Circa: 1890	375.00
Row 4, 1.	PENDANT, Gilt over brass frame w/bezel-set, hand-painted miniature portrait. Circa: 1890	150.00
Row 4, 2.	CHAIN, Low karat finely braided chain w/barrel screw clasp and gold slide set w/diamond. Circa: 1900	125.00
Row 5, 1.	PIN, Gilt over brass, twisted frame, bezel-set glass for sepia photo. Circa: 1910	65.00
Row 5, 2.	BROOCH, Gold, heavy twisted and engraved frame swivel brooch. *Front*: Man in Civil War uniform. *Back*: Same man in civilian dress. Circa: 1850	225.00
Row 5, 3.	FOB, Gold, scalloped and bezel-set 2-piece glass inserts for photo or momento. Circa: 1920	85.00

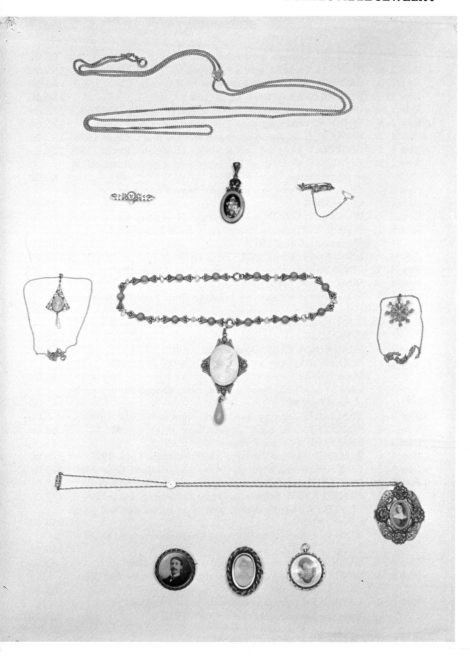

PLATE 41

From the Collections of: Baker • Kastigir • Griesman •
McDonough • Skellington

94

PLATE 42.

ROW & NO.	DESCRIPTION	VALUE
Row 1, 1.	BROOCH, Enamel, gold w/half pearls. Circa: 1890	85.00
Row 1, 2.	BROOCH, Sunburst, gold w/opals and half pearls. Circa: 1890	150.00
Row 1, 3.	BROOCH, Shell cameo in narrow filigree cage. Circa: 1900	55.00
Row 1, 4.	BROOCH, Carved ivory. Circa: 1920	150.00
Row 1, 5.	BROOCH, Gold, enamel center w/half pearls. Circa: 1860	125.00
Row 1, 6.	BROOCH, Gold w/opals. Circa: 1880	125.00
Row 1, 7.	BROOCH, Gold, *baroque* w/opals and half pearls. Circa: 1880	125.00
Row 2, 1.	BRACELET, Gold links set w/stones (1 of pair). Circa: 1890	250.00
Row 2, 2.	BRACELET, Gold bangle w/etruscan-type ornamentation set w/paste stones. Circa: 1910	65.00
Row 2, 3.	BRACELET, Cuff-type, pink gold, heavily engraved. Circa: 1890	135.00
Row 2, 4.	BRACELET, Gold links set w/stones (1 of pair). Circa: 1890	250.00
Row 3, 1.	BEADS, Cut crystals, rondell-type, (colorless quartz), Bohemian. Circa: 1925	150.00
Row 3, 2.	RING, Coral cameo, gold. Circa: 1870	175.00
Row 3, 3.	RING, Sterling, bloodstone, marcasites. Circa: 1930	85.00
Row 3, 4.	RING, Carved coral, gold. Circa: 1870	135.00
Row 3, 5.	RING, *Baroque* engraving set w/opal and *pavé* set diamonds. Circa: 1900	250.00
Row 3, 6.	RING, Gold, set w/varied cabochon-cut gemstones (Nepal). Circa: 1950	150.00
Row 3, 7.	RING, Cripple Creek Gold. Circa: 1950	75.00
Row 4, 1.	ACCESSORY, Coin holder, sterling, w/loop for chain. Circa: 1895	85.00
Row 4, 2.	VANITY LOCKET, Small powder case, silverplate, w/loop for chain. Circa: 1910	95.00
Row 4, 3.	BRACELET, Cuff-type, gold wash, engraved. Circa: 1900	65.00
Row 4, 4.	BRACELET, Gold wash bangle. Circa: 1900	45.00
Row 4, 5.	BRACELET, Gold wash bangle. Circa: 1900	45.00
Row 4, 6.	BRACELET, Plastic set w/topaz-color rhinestones. Circa: 1925	75.00
Row 4, 7.	WATCH, Woman's, Waltham, sterling case and chain. Circa: 1889	325.00
Row 5, 1.	BRACELET, Gold wash, spiral-spring coil. Circa: 1930	45.00
Row 5, 2.	BRACELET, Gold, cuff-type, w/filigree and beading. Circa: 1870	225.00
Row 5, 3.	BRACELET, Narrow circlet, gold set w/rubies and half pearls. Circa: 1870	250.00
Row 6, 1.	PENDANT, Carved ivory in gold bead frame w/gold chain. Circa: 1870	175.00
Row 6, 2.	EARRINGS, Cut crystal on gold wire. Circa: 1880	85.00
Row 6, 3.	PENDANT, Etched crystal in sterling frame w/sterling link chain. Circa: 1900	85.00
Row 6, 4.	*LAVALIERE, Art Nouveau*, gold w/opal and half pearls and *Baroque* pearl w/gold chain. Circa: 1910	325.00

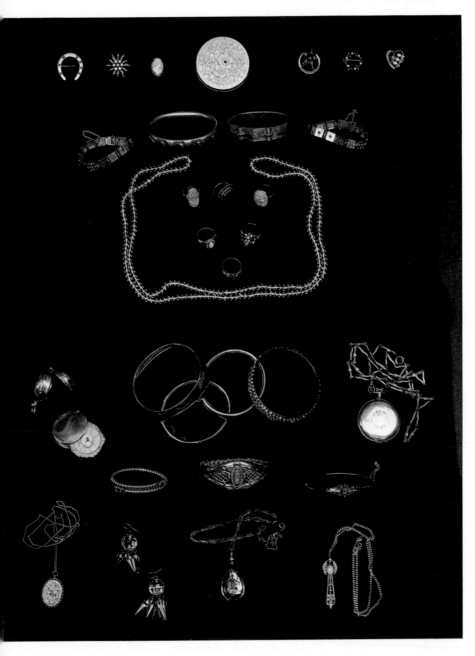

PLATE 42
From the Collections of: Toombs • Baker • Barlow • Roth

PLATE 43.

ROW & NO.	DESCRIPTION	VALUE
Row 1, 1.	BEADS, Cut and faceted amber. Circa: 1920	250.00
Row 1, 2.	BEADS, Venetian iridescent beads. Circa: 1925	125.00
Row 1, 3.	PENDANT, Raw amber w/embedded insect. Circa: 1920	125.00
Row 1, 4.	NECKLACE, Gold wash filigree w/Bohemian pink faceted glass. Circa: 1930	75.00
Row 1, 5.	NECKLACE, Three-strand branch coral bits. Circa: 1920	135.00
Row 1, 6.	BROOCH, Gold w/branch coral. Circa: 1910	55.00
Row 1, 7.	BROOCH, Gold heart w/branch coral. Circa: 1910	55.00
Row 1, 8.	BROOCH, Rolled gold wire w/branch coral. Circa: 1910	35.00
Row 1, 9.	BAR PIN, Gold etruscan-type, w/rose-cut diamond. Circa: 1880	110.00
Row 1, 10.	WATCH FOB, W/vest chain, gold wash. Circa: 1915	65.00
Row 1, 11.	WATCH FOB, Signet-type w/escutcheon, gold wash. Circa: 1915	75.00
Row 1, 12.	WATCH FOB, Signet-type w/escutcheon, gold wash. Circa: 1915	65.00
Row 1, 13.	WATCH CHAIN, Gold, unusual links. Circa: 1930	85.00
Row 1, 14.	WATCH CHAIN, Gold w/enameled fraternal emblem (32nd degree Mason). Circa: 1935	110.00
Row 1, 15.	WATCH PIN, Gold w/black enamel, set w/half pearls. Circa: 1910	95.00
Row 2, 1.	BELT BUCKLES, Signed Oriental *Satsuma*-ware. Circa: 1910	225.00
Row 2, 2.	SCARF PIN, Gold, set w/opal and diamonds. Circa: 1915	110.00
Row 2, 3.	BRACELET, Gold link w/8 charms in gold and precious stones. Circa: 1930	425.00
Row 2, 4.	BRACELET, Sterling w/synthetic sapphires. Circa: 1910	65.00
Row 2, 5.	BRACELET, Sterling w/gold wash w/cut amethyst Bohemian glass. Circa: 1920	65.00
Row 2, 6.	BRACELET, Oxidized metal w/gold coins. Circa: 1930	125.00
Row 2, 7.	BEADS, Venetian cut amberina glass beads. Circa: 1925	125.00
Row 3, 1.	LOCKET, Three-color gold wash combined in vine w/wax-bead pearls. Circa: 1900	65.00
Row 3, 2.	LOCKET, Gold wash w/garnets. Circa: 1880	85.00
Row 3, 3.	BROOCH, *Art Nouveau* moth design w/simulated stones, gold wash. Circa: 1915	75.00
Row 3, 4.	WATCH PIN, Gold *Art Nouveau*. Circa: 1910	75.00
Row 3, 5.	BROOCH, Pink shell cameo in engraved gold frame. Circa: 1900	65.00
Row 3, 6.	BROOCH, Gold *Art Nouveau*. Circa: 1910	75.00
Row 3, 7.	BROOCH, Child's brooch w/escutcheon for engraving. Circa: 1910	25.00
Row 3, 8.	BROOCH, Enamel on sterling. Circa: 1900	45.00
Row 3, 9.	LORGNETTE GLASSES, Spectacles as *lorgnette* w/gold frame and chain. Circa: 1925	175.00
Row 4, 1.	EARRINGS, Faceted French Jet w/gold wire. Circa: 1880	35.00
Row 4, 2.	EARRINGS, Etruscan-type gold w/enamel and half pearls w/gold wire. Circa: 1880	125.00
Row 4, 3.	EARRINGS, Gold enamel w/gold wire. Circa: 1890	75.00
Row 4, 4.	EARRINGS, Gold love-birds, engraved, 2-color green and yellow gold w/gold wire. Circa: 1900	75.00
Row 4, 5.	EARRINGS, French Jet glass tear-drop w/gold wire. Circa: 1880	75.00
Row 4, 6.	EARRINGS, Gold w/black enamel w/gold wire. Circa: 1850	100.00
Row 5, 1.	EARRINGS, Black & white onyx cameo, gold w/gold wire. Circa: 1885	150.00
Row 5, 2.	BROOCH, Sterling w/sapphire, *Art Nouveau*. Circa: 1910	65.00
Row 5, 3.	BROOCH, Sterling child's pin. Circa: 1910	25.00
Row 5, 4.	FOUR CHARMS, Sterling and enamel, Christian symbols: Cross and "Faith, Hope, Charity." Circa: 1890	150.00
Row 5, 5.	BROOCH, Wooden, hand-cut from Americus wood/Kansas, by Marlow, simulated Wedgwood silhouette. Circa: 1935	35.00

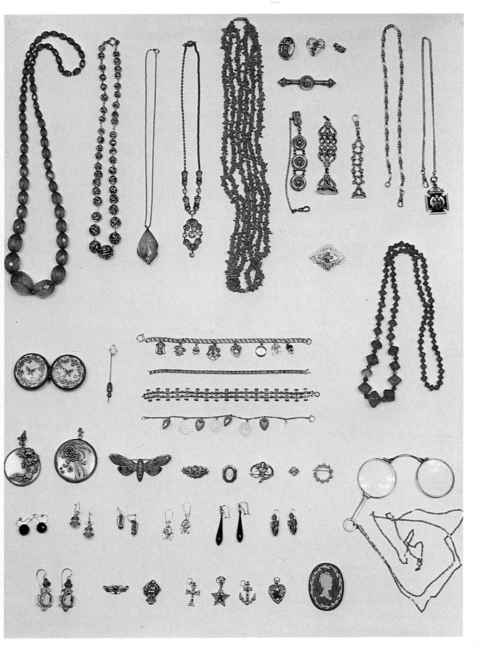

PLATE 43

From the Collections of: Toombs • Baker • Roth

PLATE 44.

ROW & NO.	DESCRIPTION	VALUE

Top to Bottom.

1. HAT ORNAMENT, 4¾" overall ornament set w/rhinestones and simulated pearls. Circa: 1925 — 65.00

2. HAT ORNAMENT, 3½" overall size w/pearl and Peking glass accented by rhinestones. Circa: 1925 — 55.00

3. HAT ORNAMENT, 5½" overall size sword marked: "© *Florenza.*" Circa: 1950 — 75.00

4. HAT ORNAMENT, 3½" overall size, abstract floral design set w/ imitation stones. Circa: 1935 — 45.00

5. HAT ORNAMENT, 4½" overall size, plastic w/simulated stones. Circa: 1935 — 75.00

PLATE 44
From the Collection of: Baker

PLATE 45.

ROW & NO.	DESCRIPTION	VALUE
Row 1, 1.	WATCH PIN, Gold plated w/simulated rose zircon, cabochon cut. Circa: 1900	55.00
Row 1, 2.	CROSS, Gold plated w/simulated rose zircons. Circa: 1900	35.00
Row 1, 3.	CROSS, Gold w/topaz-color citrine stones. Circa: 1900	75.00
Row 1, 4.	SLIDE, Large, heavy gold, for fan chain. Initial set with cut jet and agate. (Rare). Circa: 1880	135.00
Row 1, 5.	LOCKET, Gold wash set w/Persian turquoise. Circa: 1850	125.00
Row 1, 6.	BROOCH, Garnets in oxidized metal, sunburst. Circa: 1900	125.00
Row 2, 1.	BROOCH, *Art Nouveau*, oxidized silver, set w/citrine-color stone. Circa: 1910	85.00
Row 2, 2.	FUR CLIP, Double prong-spring fuchsia, enamel w/rhinestones-- for fur, pelt or hat. Circa: 1930	135.00
Row 2, 3.	BROOCH, Fine French paste, *baroque* design. Circa: 1900	75.00
Row 2, 4.	SASH ORNAMENT, *Art Nouveau*, gold wash, simulated hasp set w/simulated stones. Circa: 1910	65.00
Row 3, 1.	BANGLE BRACELETS, Souvenir-type, brass w/gold wash, handmade for fairs and expositions. Circa: 1935	set 85.00
Row 3, 2.	BROOCH, Gold wash on sterling, filigree w/branch coral on gold wires. Circa: 1900	110.00
Row 3, 3.	BRACELET, Cuff-type, gold w/black enamel. Circa: 1870	125.00
Row 3, 4.	BRACELET, Sterling, clasped hands. (Rare find). Circa: 1895	110.00
Row 4, 1.	PENCIL, Silver over nickel, engraved w/chain. Circa: 1910	65.00
Row 4, 2.	ACCESSORY, Powder case, sterling, monogrammed, w/loop for chain, Circa: 1893	85.00
Row 4, 3.	LIPSTICK VANITY, Engraved sterling w/synthetic garnet. Circa: 1930	65.00
Row 4, 4.	COIN PURSE, Cut steel and silver, *baroque*. Circa: 1890	75.00
Row 4, 5.	*CHATELAINE* PURSE, Sterling mesh on chain. Circa: 1895	110.00
Row 4, 6.	TASSEL, Sterling w/loop to hang on chain. Circa: 1890	35.00
Row 4, 7.	MONEY CLIP, Rhodium w/rhinestones. Circa: 1930	35.00

PLATE 45

From the Collection of: Peery

PLATE 46.

ROW & NO.	DESCRIPTION	VALUE
Row 1.	HATPINS, Gift-boxed, removable and interchangeable heads, enamel w/French paste stones. Circa: 1900	425.00
Row 2.	HATPINS, Hinged-head w/mother-of-pearl and seed pearls. Patented "point-protectors". Matching studs and collar pin. Circa: 1900	475.00
Row 3. Left	HATPINS, Pair, gold, w/matching veil pins. Circa: 1885	385.00
Row 3. Right	HATPINS, Pair, gold, set w/Persian turquoise. Circa: 1890	325.00
Row 4.	HATPINS, Hinged-heads, enamel on sterling w/matching studs and sash buckle. Circa: 1900	550.00

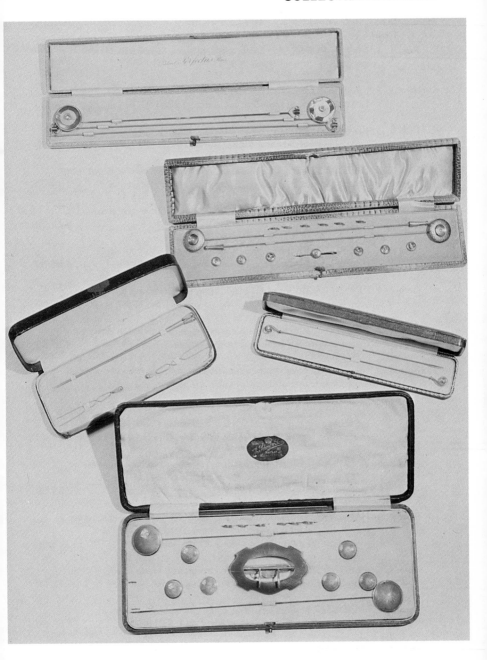

PLATE 46
From the Collections of: Baker • Alexander

PLATE 47.

ROW & NO.	DESCRIPTION	VALUE

Top to Bottom

Row 1, 1. VANITY PURSE, *Art Deco*, plastic, black geometric design set w/rhinestones. Circa: 1925 — 250.00

Row 1, 2. VANITY PURSE, *Art Deco*, plastic, rectangular-shaped French Ivory set w/glass imitation jet. Circa: 1925 — 150.00

Row 1, 3. VANITY PURSE, *Art Deco*, plastic, rectangular w/glass imitation emeralds and topaz. Circa: 1925 — 185.00

Row 2, 1. HANDBAG, Victorian, black satin w/jet glass beads, floral motif, sterling frame, engraved "*Edith F. Morris.*" Circa: 1890 — 150.00

Row 2, 2. COIN PURSE, Victorian, sterling, cupid motif w/cut steel beads. Circa: 1898 — 125.00

Row 2, 3. HANDBAG, Victorian, gun metal color velvet w/cut steel beads, 9-ball fringe w/self-loop handle. Circa: 1895 — 110.00

Row 2, 4. POUCH BAG, Victorian, black crochet drawstring w/jet glass large-cut beads w/beaded fringe drops. Circa: 1900 — 85.00

Row 3, 1. HANDBAG, *Whiting-Davis* silver mesh, enameled w/enameled frame w/detailed basket of flowers motif. Circa: 1910 — 450.00

Row 3, 2. HANDBAG, Rose velvet w/pearls and gold-color beads w/gold embossed frame and griffin chain loops. Circa: 1910 — 325.00

Row 3, 3. HANDBAG, *Whiting-Davis* silver mesh, brown and blue w/white geometric zigzag enamel w/blue and white Peking glass cabochons, trumpet lily motifs in frame. Circa: 1910 — 425.00

Row 3, 4. HANDBAG, Fine crystal beads on beige w/red rose beaded motif w/gilt frame w/carnelian clasp, multi-enamel and imitation lapis beads. Circa: 1910 — 325.00

Row 3, 5. HANDBAG, Stitched embroidery on black taffeta w/elaborate frame, engraved w/matching chain w/*Art Deco* clasp set w/imitation Peking glass stones. Circa: 1910 — 225.00

Row 3, 6. HANDBAG, *Art Nouveau* silver frame and chain w/aqua shantung fabric. Circa: 1910 — 275.00

Row 3, 7. HANDBAG, Mustard crochet square w/blue crystal beads, gilt filigree frame w/ornate clasp. Circa: 1910 — 150.00

Row 3, 8. HANDBAG, Victorian, gilt frame, gothic figurals as clasp, paisley w/cut steel beads, matching coin purse insert. Circa: 1900 — 425.00

PLATE 47

From the Collections of: Western Costume Co. • Whittier

PLATE 48.

ROW & NO.	DESCRIPTION	VALUE

L-R.

1.   *FINGER CHATELAINE*, For grooming. (Chinese) Silver w/bells and w/implements to clean ears, nose, teeth, and fingernails. Circa: 1880   225.00

2.   BRACELET, Cinnabar and filigree sterling silver. Circa: 1920   135.00

3.   NECKLACE, 18K gold, hand-linked chain, w/14K Foo Dog; Chinese burial piece (under tongue); charms (gold and jade); bird (1930). Large jade celestial w/drop. Jades are in Imperial, mutton, amethyst, and apple-green colors. Circa: 1885   3,200.00

4.   RING, Jade in Mandarin setting, 18K gold, Chinese lettering. Circa: 1895   850.00

"...The Chinese loved jade. That strange lump of stone with its faintly muddy light, like the crystallized air of the centuries, melting dimly, dully back, deeper and deeper – are not we Orientals the only ones who know its charm? We cannot say ourselves what it is that we find in this stone. Its quiet lacks the brightness of a ruby or an emerald or the glitter of a diamond. But this much we can say: when we see that shadowy surface, we think how Chinese it is, we seem to find in cloudiness the accumulated sediment of the long Chinese past, we think how appropriate it is that the Chinese should admire that surface and that shadow."

(*In Praise of Shadows*, Tanizaki Junichiro (1934), from Edward Seidensticker's adaptation, *Atlantic Monthly Supplement, Perspective of Japan*, January 1955.)

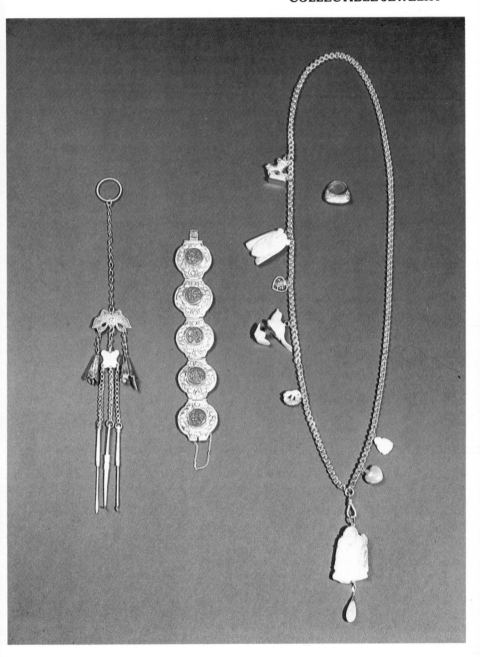

PLATE 48
From the Collection of: Peery

PLATE 49.

ROW & NO.	DESCRIPTION	VALUE
Row 1, 1.	JEWEL BOX, French Ivory w/velvet, gilt on brass, *baroque* clasp/latch. Circa: 1930	110.00
Row 1,2.	JEWEL BOX, Ceramic transfer, (F. Boucher), hand-painted porcelain, gilt on brass fittings. Marked: *Made in France, expressly for Marshall Field & Co.; Chicago*". Circa: 1895	225.00
Row 2, 1	JEWEL BOX, Heart-shaped gothic design in brass and bronze. Circa: 1890	95.00
Row 2, 2.	JEWEL BOX, *Art Nouveau*, footed, bronze. Circa: 1895	150.00
Row 2, 3.	JEWEL BOX, *Art Nouveau*, footed, heart-shaped, bronze. Circa: 1895	135.00
Row 3, 1.	JEWEL BOX, Paper transfer print under glass, gilt on brass, silk lined. High relief braid and floral pattern. Circa: 1880	110.00
Row 3, 2.	JEWEL BOX, Lacquered black walnut w/ivory clasp and hand-painted scene on ivory. Circa:1880	225.00
Row 3, 3.	JEWEL BOX, Gilt and enamel transfer portrait signed *"LeBrun"*, velvet lined (France). Circa: 1890	185.00
Row 4, 1.	JEWEL BOX, Italian mosaic crucifix or stamp box. Circa: 1900	110.00
Row 4, 2.	JEWEL BOX, Bronze collar-button box w/collar-button atop as part of overall design. Circa: 1910	150.00
Row 4, 3.	JEWEL BOX, Gilt on brass w/paper transfer under glass. Circa: 1900	85.00
Top 1.	PENCIL, Gold plated w/*grosgrain* ribbon w/gold plated slide bar. Circa: 1925	65.00
2.	PENCIL, Silver, w/*grosgrain* ribbon w/silver slide buckle. Circa: 1925	65.00
3.	BEADS, Amethyst quartz beads w/silk tassels. Circa: 1920	150.00
Bottom 1.	OPERA GLASSES, Snail-shell covered, gold plated fittings w/detachable *lorgnette*, loop for *chatelaine* chain. Circa: 1920	275.00
2.	CUFF LINKS, *Top*: Gold, engraved. *Middle*: Snail-shell in sterling. *Bottom*: Burnished gold. Circa: 1910-1920	pr. 45.00
3.	BRACELET, Victorian, gold link chain w/lock. Circa: 1900	350.00

PLATE 49

From the Collections of: Whittier • Biddle • A. Fries •
Henning • Baker • Western Costume Co.

SECTION 3

GLOSSARY of jewelry *terms* and
jewelry *types,* including *pronunciations.*

GLOSSARY OF JEWELRY TERMS AND TYPES
INCLUDING PRONUNCIATIONS

ABALONE, -ab-ŏ-lŏ-nē,
>Sea-shell creature of the Pacific Coast with an inner-shell lining of gray/pink natural pearlized substance.

ACCESSORIES
>Jeweled accessories played a prominent part in the late 19th and 20th Century costume. They held the unique position of being useful jewelry, combining beauty and utility. The useful articles included the memorandum tablet, the *lorgnette, the chatelaine,* buckles, hatpins, fashionable fans, pocket opera glasses, buckles, and sash pins, and the various beaded bags and purses. The *chatelaines* were equipped with several chains to accommodate the following "necessaries": coin purses, vanity cases in the form of lockets for powder puffs and mirrors, silver card cases, a pencil, a place for lip salve, *vinaigrettes,* a bon bon box for scent pills, and a tiny writing tablet. These accessories added an intangible expression of charm to the individual costume.

AGATE
>A variety of quartz or natural gemstone, the most common being the banded or striped agate. Among the varieties of quartz known as agate, is black onyx often used for cameos and *intaglios.* The carnelian or red agate is prized for beads and *intaglio* seals. Moss-colored agate or gray-striped agate from Scotland was very popular during Victorian times while Brazilian agates and those mined in India contribute to today's requirements for mass-produced jewelry.

AIGRETTE, -ā'gret
>A hair ornament with a plume or spray most often accentuated by either a jewel or buckle.

AMBER
>A yellowish-brown fossil resin. This fossilized resin, also found in black and varieties of brown and orange, comes from ancient forests of fir trees or mined from under the Baltic Sea. The orange-color amber comes from Sicily.

·**AMETHYST**
>A gemstone in shades from pale lavender to deep purple found in Russia, Brazil, Uruguay, Ceylon, and the United States.

ARABESQUES, - ār'ab-esk
>Flowing scrollwork in line, leaves, curlicues, etc., often in low relief.

ART DECO (1910-1930)
>A stilted, stylized design, a transition from *Art Nouveau,* which found its influence in the 1925 *"L'Exposition Internationale des Arts Decoratifs et Industriels Modernes",* (Paris 1925), as well as in the art of the American Indian, ancient Egyptians, and in Greek and Roman architecture. Early '20's interest in Cubism as a new art form also influenced the design of the *Art Deco* Period. The King Tut traveling exhibit (1977), has renewed the craze for Egyptian-

designed jewelry. Additionally, there is more interest than ever in the mysteries of the Pyramids and a continuing revival of astrology which lends itself to *Art Deco* design.

ART MODERNE (1935-1945)

It is generally accepted that the period of the 1920's to the 1930's is the *Art Deco* Period. The decade of the '40's and '50's is considered the "modern" period, a period in which just about any conceivable type of design--whether it be flamboyant or contrived with delicate fancy--survived. The *Art Moderne* Period (1935-1945) avoids frivolous swirls and instead "streamlines" into crisp, geometric lines. "Modern" seems to be a word which gives license to all creativity in any form, be it eccentric or strictly along conventional jeweler's lines. The *Art Moderne* Period expresses the conflict between machine and nature which is evident in *Art Deco*; but *Art Moderne* contains somewhat less artistry and some pieces appear as absurdities. Most *Art Moderne* jewelry combines phenolics and modern metals such as chrome and rhodium. However, there have been great jewelry pieces executed in 3-dimensional *Art Moderne* form designed by famed artists, Georges Braque and Salvador Dali.

ART NOUVEAU (1890-1910), - *art nu-vo*

A short-lived art style introduced in the late 19th Century and ending in the early 20th, its jewelry designs, incorporated undulating curves, spirals, and flowing lines. The influence of the Japanese art form is most apparent and was popularized by the 1876 trade between Japan and the western lands. *Art Nouveau* was known in other countries as follows:

AMERICA, ENGLAND, and FRANCE: *L'Art Nouveau* for the Paris establishment of Samuel Bing (1895).

BOHEMIA: "Recession" or "Seccession".

GERMANY: *"Jugenstil"*, after the art magazine called "Jugend", meaning "youth".

ITALY: *"Stile Liberty"*, after London's Liberty & Co., Regent Street, Department Store.

SPAIN: *"Arte Joven"*, meaning "young art".

The *Art Nouveau* jewelers incorporated the sinuous lines of the female figure and nature's curlicues which are found in florals. They grasped in graphics the imaginative, flighty, fancifull, ornate butterflies, birds, and creatures of fantasy worlds...*Art Nouveau* is fantasy personified.

Art Nouveau profoundly stirred the imagination of artists in every line of endeavor. The *Art Nouveau* jewelers executed pieces showing women with flowing locks; florals that seemed moved by some invisible wind; insects that discarded their biological garb and embraced the once-scorned "inferior" gemstones.

Art Nouveau reached its height by 1900, being pushed from the scene with the advent of worldwide social and political upheaval. But this brief encounter with such giants as America's Louis Comfort Tiffany, Austria's Gustave Limpt, Belguim's Velde and Horta, England's C.R. Ashby and William Morris, and the greatest genius of them all, Rene' Lalique of France, left an impression which is just recently being felt and appreciated by both professionals and laymen alike.

The birthplace of *Art Nouveau* was the 1888 School of Handicraft established by Charles Robert Ashby and William Morris, in Great Britian. They, in turn, influenced Walter Crane (1880) and John Ruskin, his contemporary, and that unpredictable virtuoso of pen and ink, Aubrey Beardsley.

114

It all began in Britain--despite the French moniker--with Matthew Boulton's Victorian pieces being challenged by the *Art Nouveau* jewelers and artists who were followers of Morris and Ashby.

BAGS (see PURSES)

BAGUETTE, - bă-gĕt'
A narrow rectangular-cut stone most often chosen for diamonds. The baguette cut was influenced by the interest in Cubism of the 1920's. When associated with emeralds it is called "emerald-cut".

BAKELITE
A trade-mark for a synthetic resin chemically formulated and named after Belgian chemist, L.H. Backeland, (1909). It is for molding items formerly created in Celluloid or hard rubber. A much more recent type of plastic is known as Lucite. Bakelite is opaque whereas Lucite is usually transparent or translucent.

BAROQUE, - bă-rōk'
Bold, ornate, heavy-looking ornamentation.

BARRETT
Another name for barrett is hair clasp, particularly those into which a beautiful silk or *grosgrain* ribbon bow could be inserted. They were available in elegant gold or silver plate, highly chased and engraved and some were also offered in sterling silver and solid gold. Metallic barretts were marketed from 1895 through 1910; through the '20's they were made not only of metals, but of plastic. Most barretts were either engraved or chased and were set with rhinestones, gems, and gemstones. Sterling barretts were more popular after the 1930's.

BEAD
An ornament with a hole end to end into which a needle can be inserted. Most glass beads came from Czechoslavakian, Italian, and American glass-blowing factories. Beads are made from gemstones, metals, shells, seeds, ivory, bone, stone, or horn. Glass beads are made on a blowing rod and then pierced. Home-crafted beads were fashioned from colorful wallpaper and paste by Victorian damsels interested in "parlor work".

BEZEL
A groove or flange which holds a stone secure in its setting.

BELTS
Metallic belts and large metal buckles were popular during the latter part of the 18th Century and then again in the 1930's and '40's. During the Victorian Era, the metal belts, often made in solid gold, were used to accentuate a small waist. The chasing and engraving on the metal was executed so as to pick up the pattern of the lace on the garment being worn.

BIRTHSTONE JEWELRY (see GEMS)

BLACK GLASS JEWELRY (see JET)
Imitation jet or onyx.

BOG OAK
A dark brown peat-like material used especially by the Irish for inexpensive jewelry. It is a carved material and is not molded.

BOX SETTING
A stone enclosed in a box-shaped setting with edges of metal pressed down to hold it in place. (Also called "Gypsy" setting.)

BRACELETS
Bracelets have been popular since time immemorial. The 100 years (1850-1950) produced "jointed" wide-cuffed bracelets and unjointed bangle-type bracelets, the latter often given in friendship. Adjustable bracelets were worn by both ladies and infants and had an adjustable "expando" mechanism. Because Queen Victoria's Prince Consort presented her with a wedding ring in the form of two serpents entwining, bracelets with this motif were very much in vogue during her long reign. With the discovery of King Tut's tomb, the serpent again became symbols in many pieces of jewelry, and most eloquently in the bracelets of the *Art Deco* Period. Link bracelets with charms dangling from each link were the rage in the 1900's to 1905 and then reappeared in popularity in the 1930's. The charms were represented as hearts, clovers, etc., many engraved with the donor's initials. With a lock and key, the link bracelet was another popular conceit of the Victorian Era. There was great variation and artistry in the linkage and in the variety of shape and design of both lock and key. Bracelets made of mesh were also designed with lock and key and usually ended with one or more delightful tassels hanging at the closure. The bangle bracelet was originally called a "bangle ring" although it was made to fit around the wrist. It resembled an enlarged ring and was called a "bangle ring" because the wire was very narrow and resembled a wedding band. The adjustable cuff or band bracelet was another innovation of the 1890's, as was the coil or mesh wire bracelet available in gold plate or rolled gold. The coil bracelets were adjustable in that being a coil, they could be stretched. The wedding band type of bracelet could also be expanded with either end separating and then popping together after it was placed on the wrist. From 1850 to 1910 the "stiff band" or cuff bracelet was preferred and was from 1" to 2" wide, set with precious gems and gemstones. High relief and much black tracery enamel work were featured on the cuff bracelets.

BRASS
Yellowish-gold color which is primarily an alloy of copper, tin, zinc, or other base metal.

BRILLIANTS
Another term for paste, *strass*, or rhinestones.

BROOCH (see PINS)

BUCKLES
Buckles were wrought for belt, sash, shoes, capes and hats. The simulated belt buckle was actually a brooch with a simulated hasp that was pinned in front of a sash, belt, or shirtwaist. They were finished in Roman gold, rose gold, antique gold, silver, French grey, oxidized metals, and in gun metal. Buckles were fashionable on belts after the turn-of-the-century. When the belt buckle

was designed to meet at an angle rather than in a horizontal manner, they were called the "new dip" belt buckle. Shirtwaists were "in" at this same period and women demanded buckles that matched pins, studs, as well as hatpins and collar stays. Colonial-type shoe buckles came in oxidized silver and were used to accent a brown or black calfskin pump with a very high tongue. The clasp of the tongue fit into the colonial buckle, and the shoe was called "Colonial pump" because this type buckle was a reproduction of the earlier fashions. Many colonial-type shoe buckles were of beautiful cut steel. The color of the metal was called "French Grey," often had hand-etching, and was usually square. However, this soon gave way to many new shapes, particularly the oblong. In the 1915-1925 era there was a new color called "brown jewelry" which was a kind of seal-brown tone of metal and went very well with the popular brown fabric which was becoming the vogue at the beginning of the 20th Century. With the demise of Queen Victoria, brown had come into fashion as well as French Grey. Around the second and third decades of the 20th Century, the simulated sash buckle with the simulated hasp was introduced and worn on the wider cumberbund-type belts which were worn rather closer to the hips than to the waist. During the reign of Empress Eugenie (France), belts at the waistline were very much in vogue. The Empress had a beautiful figure and naturally wanted to accentuate her very small waistline. Small waists were in until after WWI when the flapper girl costume brought the so-called waistline to well below the curve of the hip.

BUTTONS, (Dress)

Women's dress buttons came in sets of three and were joined by a very delicate lovely link chain which prevented loss. The stud end was worn inside the blouse which, before 1900, was called a "waist". The waist was called a "shirt" from 1900 to 1920 and then a "blouse". Dress buttons were beautifully engraved with raised borders and were set with garnets, or pearls, or turquoise. The same sets of dress buttons were made in miniature for children's wear. In most cases, unlike women's dress buttons, children's button sets were made not only in threes but in fours. The children's button sets were much more simple in design, with a ribbed or polished front and occasionally set with a very small half-pearl or garnet. Children's and women's dress buttons came in many shapes: bar shape, oblong shape, and oval shape. Others had beautiful curved designs wonderfully engraved with lovely rippled or ribbed cable patterns.

CABOCHON, - kà-bŏ-shŏn'

A stone without facets shaped like a dome.

CAIRNGORM, kârn'gorm'

Yellow or smokey brown clear quartz mined especially in Cairngorm, Scotland, and featured in the Scottish brooches and jeweled accessories.

CAMEO

Conch shell, onyx gem, or coral, carved in relief. Also in molded synthetics and glass.

CARAT (English) or KARAT (American)

Standard unit of weight for gems, or a measure for gold tabled at 1/24th part of pure gold in an alloy.

The term *carat* as a symbol for unit weight of gems and gemstones: (ct.) 1 ct. diamond = 1 ct.

The symbol *k-* used for gold: 24 *k* = 18 parts gold to 6 parts alloy, on so forth down the scale.

Carat marks began about 1890. European carat marks were: 9, 15, or 18. American jewelry was primarily 14 karat.

10 carat gold was used for less expensive pieces and for the earlier Victorian pieces which were made before stringent hallmarking was in effect.

CARNELIAN (also called CORNELIAN)

A variety of chalcedony with a wax-like luster. A precious stone found largely in Greece or in Asia Minor, carnelian has a translucent color which may be deep red, flesh red, or reddish-white color. It takes a good polish and cut and is, therefore, ideal for seals and *intaglios*.

CARTOUCHE, - *kär-tōōsh'*

A shield or scroll with curved edges used particularly on silver for monogram, crest, or initial.

CELLULOID

A trade-mark of Hyatt Bros., Newark, N.J., (1868). It is a composition mainly of gun cotton and camphor, resembling ivory in texture and color. It is also dyed to imitate coral, tortoise-shell, amber, malachite, etc. Originally called *xylonite*, Celluloid is the word most often used to cover any imitation ivory, bone, or tortoise. But there were many other imitators such as: "ivorine", "French ivory", "tortine", and the like. Celluloid should not be confused with the harder and more resiliant plastic known as Bakelite. Celuloid, being highly flammable, lost favor to phenolic resins, plastics of the 1930's. Celluloid was first used as synthetic ivory in the manufacture of billiard balls.

CERAMIC TRANSFER

A complicated and technical procedure in which designs are engraved on a copper plate, then inked; the impression on the plate is transferred to a piece of tissue paper, then again transferred to a piece of porcelain to be decorated. The transfer design is then either left one color or hand-colored with tinting. A permanent glaze is applied, fired in the kiln, and unless the glaze is scratched, it retains the original design intact. Transfer designs were applied to brooches and hatpins, but this practice is more familiar on printed earthenware.

CHAINS

Probably the most widely used chain is the ordinary neck chain with a clasp to attach a pendant, watch, locket, medallion, etc.. When Queen Victoria married Prince Albert in 1849, immediately there was a chain named for him-- the "Albert Chain"-- which had a lapel bar on one end and swivel or tongue-pin on the other end of the chain, and was worn draped across the vest. At the center of this chain was a small jump ring which accommodated a small fob-type medallion or charm. A woman's chain of the same period was similar to the Albert Chain but much shorter and was called the "Victoria" or "Queen Chain."It usually had several charms dangling from various interruptions in the linkage. Vest chains were made mostly in solid gold, or in either 10-carat or 14-carat with a great variety of linkages. There were square, oval, flat, square twist, and ship's cable, among many others. The vest chain was popularized by the visit of Charles Dickens to this country and eventually showed up in the 1893 catalogues under "Dickens Vest Chain". Men wore their vest chains slung across the front of their vests and women's "vest chains" were smaller duplicates of the men's chains except that they were more intricately and more delicately wrought than a man's. The woman's vest chain differed in that they had slides on the chains which shortened or tightened the chain which was then draped into a belt or pinnned to the waist-shirt.

From these chains were small pendant chains on which hung charms, lockets, and vinaigrettes, all beautifully engraved and set with turquoise, pearls, or garnets. The Victoria Chains had as long a life in fashion as did the Royal Queen of England. The Victoria Chains often had as many as four or five *chatelaine* drops beginning from near the top of the cross-bar or lapel bar right to the end of the chain which fit into the belt or pinned up at the waist. Each of the *chatelaine* drops had a swivel to accommodate charms or pendants with one longer extension utilized for a watch. The vest chains for men averaged about 10" long whereas the Dickens' Vest Chains were from 13" to 15" in length. The company of Hamilton & Hamilton, Jr., (Providence, R.I.), claimed to be the first makers of gold-filled chains in America.

Neck chains for women could average as long as 48" but always included a slide which would keep the chain from slipping off the shoulder or looping a breast. There were many neck chains, some in 10 carat or 14 carat gold. The usual length of a neck chain was from 12" to 13½". Manufactured in various lengths, they came in twisted wire, woven wire, plain link chains, barrel links, chased wire, and flat links. These neck chains (or *necklaces* as they were sometimes called), were used to accommodate small charms or pendants. The pendants could well be a cross, a locket, a heart or a similar charm which satisfied the desire of the wearer. Many of the chains for men were in variations,such as double, triple and four strand vest chains, all magnificently chased and engraved and furnished with *intaglio* patterned slides. The links on the chains varied from square, round, and octagon-shape, all with chased wire or extremely fancy linkage.

Hair chains were very popular in the 1890's and real human hair was chosen in assorted dark colors. It is often difficult to distinguish real human hair from fine silk thread also woven into chains. Hair and silk jewelry had beautifully engraved findings. The only metallic portion of these chains were the five or six links which were hung by a jump-ring to a small bar that was made for insertion into the vest. At the other end of the chain was a swivel. This particular fashion of silk and human hair vest chains featured a small mounted slide about two-thirds down to the swivel from which there hung a circular linkage. From that point a charm or medallion could be displayed. The care and workmanship featured on each small finding or finishing mount brings admiration and appreciation of the jeweler's art. From 1850 to 1860 men's jewelry consisted primarily of various chains dangling fobs and watches. Eventually, fobs gave way to the Dickens' watch chains which draped across the upper torso.

CHALCEDONY, - kăl-sĕd-ŏ-nĭ

A precious stone found in Asia Minor, primarily Greece, which has a translucent quality--a variety of quartz. The term chalcedony denotes a grayish or milky-colored quartz including the family of onyx, agate, sard, cat's eye, jasper, carnelian and chrysoprase. All take high polish and are suitable for good *intaglio* work except for the cat's eye which is polished into a cabochon-cut stone.

CHANNEL SETTING

A series of stones set close together in a straight line with the sides of mounting gripping the outer edges of a stone.

CHARMS

Most charms were of low carat or gold plate. Many were set with assorted colored stones, not necessarily genuine gems. Very often Victorian charms were designed like lockets. Some could open; others had fronts that could slide out to reveal a picture of a loved one. Many lockets were of a large, thin, oval shape; some were square shaped and could open both back and front, and they were naturally of a thicker measurement. Many had a satin or high polished appearance, the satin finish look much like today's "florentine" finish. They were all highly engraved, some set with colored stones, others with an assortment of real gems.

Around 1893 some charms were actually made of solid aluminum and were guaranteed not to tarnish or corrode. They were advertised as *"...1/4 the weight of silver, five times stronger than gold".* There's no doubt that these aluminum charms, which were not hollow, could well be mistaken for silver. They were probably not as desirous as silver or sterling charms, but they represented a beautiful craft. Many of them were in the shapes of animals, and though they were of aluminum, they were still set with *genuine* garnet eyes.

Many charms, (or lockets which were worn as charms), were of rolled gold, gold front, or of rolled plate. Those that were worn by gentlemen on their watch or vest chains, were quite large and intricately worked for they were in majority made with a solid gold front. These had genuine gems set into scenic engravings with lovely chasing.

Before there were laws regarding the defacing of coinage, U.S. dimes were polished clear of engraving on one side and then newly engraved with the initials of the donor. They were called "love tokens". Christian symbols, hearts, animals, fish, fruit, clocks, insects, compasses, signets, novelties, mechanical devices, carpenter's tools, firearms, vehicles, lanterns, shoes, fraternal charms-- anything that imagination could allow -- we re the makings of Charms.

CHASING

The ornamentation of metal with grooves or lines with the use of hand-chisels and hammers. Obverse (front) chasing is called *intaglio;* chasing from reverse side (back) is called *repousse.*

CHATELAINE, - shăt́-é-lān

A decorative clasp or a hook from which many chains are hung to accommodate various household accessories or jeweler's conceits such as thimbles, scissors, keys, watches, seals, and other such decorative implements.

From the *chatelaine* also hung various "necessaries" such as a miniature fan, a glove buttoner, and a dog whistle. There were also grooming items: an ear spoon for cleaning the ears, a sharp pick for cleaning under the nails, as well as a tooth pick.

Very short *chatelaine* chains were called *chatelettes.* They measured from 2" to 6" in length. An ornamental pin or brooch was attached that it could be detached and worn separately. The *chatelette* chain had a swivel at the end of the chain from which to hang a watch. The brooch was in the popular bow-knot or pansy in magnificent *baroque* fashion or unusual twisted design. In some instances the *chatelette* chain was nothing more than two linkages with a drop swivel and resembled the more common watch pin. The clasp or hook at the head of the *chatelaine* was most often highly engraved with *baroque* or *rococo* designs. Some were set with stones but more often than not, the design was the important effect of the' *chatelaine* hook. Many used the *Fleur de Lis* motif, some a fan-shape, others ornate cherubs rendered in *baroque* fashion. The clasp-type *chatelaine* was pinned to the dress or waist, the chain dropping into a half-circle which was then joined by a swivel or snap-hook for a watch or other ornament. Ornaments could be a locket, a *vinaigrette*, a coin holder, or (as in the case of earlier *chatelaines*) little "conceits" such as the silver card case, a place for lip salve, a bon bon box for scent pills, and the like. The earliest *chatelaines* were worn at the belt-line. Victorian *chatelaines* could be worn either at the belt-line or pinned to the shirtwaist. Early 20th Century *chatelaines* were removed from the waist and there was a new introduction of a *chatelaine* ring. This ring could either be introduced to a chain or possibly even worn at the wrist.

Many *chatelaine* vanity cases came in various shapes and sizes, but ordinarily, they were similar to the gold or silver card cases which in themselves were rather comprehensive. They frequently included the puff box and the puff, pins, a little mirror, a coin compartment, memorandum tablet, and a pencil. Many of the vanity cases contained delicate traceries of enamel, some set with gems,while others had monograms engraved as part of the overall design.

The *chatelaine* is a fine example of combined beauty and utility which appeal-ed to woman's artistic sense while serving her needs.

CHOKER

A single-strand necklace or ribbon which fits snugly around the throat. The single strand could be made of pearls, gems, or beads, but could also consist of several strands of metallic chain accentuated by a central brooch. The ribbon-type choker was made of *grosgrain* or velvet. To this ribbon was added a brooch, either center or off-center, determined by the particular taste of the wearer. Both types of choker have been popular for over 100 years.

CHROME (also called CHROMIUM)

The word comes from the Greek *chroma* which means color. Chrome is a metal that forms very hard steel-gray masses which gleam a silver color. Less than 3% mixture of chromium to steel produces an extremely hard alloy; it is used for plating base metals that easily corrode. It receives it name from the green, orange, yellow, red, etc., colors which emanate from the oxide and acid which contacts specific minerals and yields chrome-green, chrome-yellow, and other color pigments. Chrome-plated jewelry is rare since it was an experimen-tal metal proving to be more expensive than silver-color platings. One may oc-casionally come upon a chrome and plastic brooch or bracelet from the *Art Deco* or *Art Moderne* Period.

CHRYSOPRASE, - kris-o-prāz

Apple-green in color, it is actually a dyed chalcedony or agate which has a cloud-like rather than brilliant color. It is almost like "vasoline" glass, seemingly with an oily surface. This stone was very popular in the *Art Nouveau* and *Art Deco* Periods.

CINNABAR

Cinnabar is the only important ore of Mercury. A brilliant red or vermilion-color mineral which is used as a red pigment. Most popular in China, the origin of the word is probably Chinese, as the color is sometimes referred to as "dragon's blood". The pigment is highly prized by Chinese artisans who use it for dying inlay-work for jewelry and other artifacts.

CITRINE
A pale lemon-colored gemstone of quartz variety often mistaken for topaz.

CLASPS
The "push-in" type clasp is the oldest form of clasp on bracelet or necklace. Brooch clasps had simple hooks under which a pin-shank was held in place; eventually safety-type devices were added. The "ball-catch" safety type of clasp consists of a 3/4 circle with a small lever-type tab which completes the round and securely locks the brooch pin. This "ball-catch" was innovated in the year 1911.

A "spring-ring" clasp is in the shape of a tiny circle with a push-pin on a spring which opens and springs shut for closure of a necklace or a bracelet. This is the most common type of clasp device.

Clasps with a chain-and-pin safety feature were worn prior to 1890, while the safety clasp mentioned above was in use after the turn-of-the-century.

Ornamental clasps were worn until the 1930's, and then came the simple, screw-barrel type, followed by a chain with an open "fish hook".

Prior to die-stamped jewelry and again in the 1930's, clasps were usually incorporated in the overall design of necklaces, pendants, chains, chokers, and bracelets. All finer designed, more expensive pieces, have such clasps.

CLAW-SET
Tiny claws or prongs curved to hold down a stone into its mounting.

CLOISONNE, - kloi-zo-na'
Enameling in which thin wire (silver, gold, bronze, or copper which has been gilded) is bent to form cells, (cloisons), then filled with enamel. Each color is in a separate compartment, each compartment separated by thin wire.

COLLAR BUTTONS & STUDS
Collar buttons were made stronger and more durable than shirt studs. That is because the collar button had to fasten the collar tightly around the throat, and collars being heavily starched, they required a strong and durable fastening.

Parks Brothers & Rogers, (Providence, R.I.), were makers of the "Parkroger", the "original...one-piece collar button, stud, and solderless cuff buttons...the original American Lever and Pointer collar buttons".

We think of the collar button as a very simple, round shape, but it actually came in many various shapes and designs; some folded forward, some were designed with Masonic symbols, some were in a pointed shape, the point often set with a pearl or diamond.

Collar buttons came with a long or short shank and many of them had patented clamps to keep them from being lost or from loosening. Some of the patented clamps opened on a small spring and had meshing teeth on either side to secure the collar.

The collar button was not only a man's accessory but a lady's as well. Ladies' collar buttons were worn in combination sets which included the collar button, dress buttons, and cuff buttons. The collar button, usually associated with men's wear, won popularity with the shirtwaist which complemented the Gibson Girl attire. Women in America took on the fashionable, masculine accessory of collar buttons, cuff buttons, and dress buttons, in matching sets, usually of rolled plate, gold or silver. All were engraved or highly chased with much raised edgework.

Dress buttons were to women what dress *studs* were to men. Studs were worn in front of the shirt and they were highly decorative. Shirt studs were commonly worn before the turn-of-the-century and even into the '20's. Today, shirt studs are usually associated with the tuxedo-front.

COMBS

Combs did not become purely ornamental until about 1880. Before that time they were not only decorative but functional. In the mid-'20's, the Gibson Girl hairdo was popular and the comb again became functional.

From 1880 to approximately 1920, the hair was arranged so as to present an attractive appearance from every viewpoint. Therefore, there was an abundance of combs, hair ornaments, flowers, etc., used to achieve this effect. Many fashion plates of the period reveal models wearing many hair combs, clasps, barretts, ribbons, etc., all at one time. No fashionable woman considered her wardrobe complete without a myriad of combs: side, pompadour, back, and purely decorative. Combs were required for various coiffures such as the Greek knot or Grecian knot which was a plain coil twisted or rolled low on the neck. This type of hairdo required hair pins as well as several fancy combs which were inserted for both utility and attractiveness.

Early combs were generally made of real tortoise-shell, bone, sterling, gold, and silver. After 1900, imitation materials were more popularly used, especially in America. Back combs usually had three or more teeth and often the crest of the comb was hinged so as to be more easily inserted and more comfortable for wearing. Fancy combs were set with brilliants and Bohemian garnets, the latter being the most desirable. Imitation tortoise-shell and ivory combs came under many trade-marks: *NuHorn, TUF-E-NUF,* and *Stag,* (manufactured (1915), by Noyes Comb Co., Binghamton, N.Y. Imitation tortoise-shell combs were manufactured by Schrader & Ehlers, N.Y., who made the "Olive Dore Combs". Sadler Bros., So. Attleboro, Mass., produced the real article of tortoise-shell as did the Wagner Comb Co. of New York. The most artful combs were imported from the Continent.

CONCEITS

A word which is used to represent curiously contrived and fanciful jewelry, or a jeweler's artifice, or jeweled accessories which are quaint, artificial, or have an affected conception which flatters one's vanity. To be *"plumed with conceit..."*, signifies an awareness or an eccentricity of dress.

The *"Delineator"* (March 1900) reported a new high fashion at the beginning of the "new century" stating that *"dainty neck conceits"* were becoming most important item in the women's wardrobe.

"...there is no bit of finery so truly feminine or possessing so many charming possibilities as the tie or collar of ribbon, velvet, chiffon or lace...". Each of these "neck conceits" was finally fastened with an unusual and attractive brooch.

Another neck conceit was a close-fitting "stock", a wide velvet ribbon folded around a stiffened foundation. Fastened on the side of the velvet ribbon was a jeweled ornament. The actual fastening of the ribbon was to the back, but the jewel pinned at the front gave the impression that the jewel was the clasp. The neck-wear of the turn-of-the-century could change waist (blouse or shirtwaist) into varied costumes to be worn with the close-fitting skirts of the period. The waistline of the skirt was accentuated with a small jeweled clasp and often that clasp would match the brooch worn at the neck or at the shoulder.

Millinery for all seasons was given brilliancy by some of the more elaborate creations and conceits of jewels such as dull gold enameling in colored alloys, crystal cabochons, wide buckles of gold, cut steel, and rhinestones. Added to all this was the ever-popular and necessary requirement, the hatpin.

The parasol was another summer-time must, many of them fascinating to see as they carried out the decoration of the smartest gowns. The handles were works of art and varied greatly in length and design. A golf-lover might have a parasol-handle in the form of a putter, wrought in gun metal; an automobile ornamentation, perhaps suggesting the make of a car, or the spokes of the wheel, could serve as the ornamental handle of another umbrella. There was no end to the designs of umbrella handles for the "sportin' woman".

One of the more unusual conceits carried by men was the physician's thermometer case which was of fine quality gold. There was a chain and pen hooked to the end piece which had a socket for the insertion of the glass thermometer. It was ornately and beautifully engraved and very often had the insignia of the *caduceus*, signifying the medical profession. This signet was comprised of a staff or wand of Hermes/Mercury, the messenger of the gods, fabled to have two serpents coiled around him. This type case was also executed in sterling silver.

Other conceits consisted of infants' and children's Bib Pins which usually measured from 1/2" to 3/4" and about 1/8" to 1/4" wide, generally of gold with enameling. The word "baby", "love", or the name of the infant or child was engraved. Another novelty conceit for children was the decorative animal pin to be worn on the lapel so the joints of the animal were rendered movable. Most were wrought in sterling silver and had a pin similar to a stickpin which was then thrust into the lapel. When the pin was worn, it moved in a live-like manner. One of the more popular of this type was the *chameleon* pin.

Several 1895 catalogues offered the following jeweled conceits: sterling encased mustache combs, ladies' hat band buckles, sterling silver hat marks, folding pocket combs, key rings, umbrella straps, bag or trunk checks, armlets or garters, and glove buttoners--all in beautifully engraved sterling silver.

CORAL

Skelton of the coral polyp. Victorian jewelry abounds with Mediterranean coral which reached its peak of popularity from 1850-1870. Interest has renewed in recent years. Iron oxide produces various shades of coral: white, pale-pink, orange, and dark red. More rarely found are yellow, blue, and black. Most desirable coral is angel-pink (pale flesh color), and deep red. Branch coral bits were used in tiny brooches or lace pins. Coral makes handsome carved cameos. Waist sets or "beauty pins" were made of branch coral and came in sets of three, each set sold on a card. Several variations of branch coral are shown in both earring drops and pins in the Montgomery Ward & Co. 1894-95 catalogue.

CORONAL

An arrangement of flowers or jewels worn as a crown.

CRYSTAL

A colorless quartz most often implemented in cut and faceted beads, pendants, and rings. Crystal, in its natural form, is not to be confused with man-made glass.

Czechoslavakian "sunray" cyrstals were set into silver or gold filigree as pendants, bracelets, rings, and earrings. In the center of the "sun" was a small set consisting of a half-pearl or diamond ordinarily outlined in a tiny filigree frame.

CUT STEEL
Beads often mistaken for marcasite.

DAMASCENE, dăm'-à-sēn
To inlay gold and silver into iron or steel in a decorative pattern. It is work which is characteristic of ornaments from the Syrian city, Damascus, famous for its steel.

DIAMONDS
A valuable gem of extreme hardness, usually clear and transparent but sometimes yellow, blue, green, or black, consisting of pure carbon.

From 1850-1900, the old mine-cut or rose-cut diamonds were in vogue. The "brilliant-cut" has 58 or more facets and relates to more modern faceting which became popular after 1918, particularly following the emphasis on creative gem-cutting by the exhibit held at the *Museum of Modern Art* (1946), and the DeBeers Consolidated Mines, Ltd., premiering of *"Diamond U.S.A. Awards"* (1954).

In 1922 the *baguette* and emerald-cut for diamonds was introduced, and the square and rectangular cuts in 1940. This was followed by the *marquis* and pear cuts which dominated the 1950's.

Pave'-set diamonds is probably the oldest form of setting for this precious gem.

DIE STAMPING
To cut a design into metal for mass-production and reproduction. This superseded hand-wrought and custom-made jewelry pieces for "the masses". Custom jewelry is considered for the "carriage trade", although *hand-wrought* has become much in demand today. Today with so many jewelry-making "novices", much hand-crafted work is reaching the general public.

DEPOSE', -dĕ-pōz'
A French word similar to the U.S. "copyright" or "patent".

DRAGON'S BREATH
Simulated Mexican fire opals, made of glass, popular from 1910-1930.

EARRINGS
Earrings are rather easily dated: the earliest were lightweight, hollow-gold, and were made with wire hooks which went through pierced ears lobes. Wire posts were in after 1900.

From 1900-1930 there were screw-backs and after 1930, the ear clip was introduced.

Fancy "pierceless" eardrops gained popularity by 1930; prior to this time most women wore pierced earrings, primarily studs and/or with short drops.

Pierceless eardrops were offered in sterling silver with imitation stones such as "French pearls", imitation coral and paste "brilliants".

Platinum had come into its own, and the following appeared in a 1913 jeweler's catalogue: " . .imitation platinum with ruby doublets and fine French pearls . . ."

Long tassel earrings were high-style during 1920-1930.

Today, all types and shapes of earrings are worn, depending on one's personality and costume.

EBONY
The word in Hebrew, (*eben*), signifies *a stone* because of its hardness and weight. Ebony is a black-colored wood of great hardness, heavier than water and capable of taking on a fine polish. It is found primarily in Ceylon and makes exquisite beads and other wooden work.

EDWARDIAN ERA (1901-1910)
The reign of Edward VII, which departed from Victorianism into an opulent, elegant period which was contrasted by a challenge to social values between British classes. The elegance in costume witnessed millinery magic, resulting in the "glory" of the hatpin era as well as the greatest innovations of *Art Nouveau* jewelry.

ELECTROPLATING (or ELECTRO-PLATING)
A process which produced great quantities of gold jewelry and replaced the former "pinchbeck" which was an imitation gold. The plating is achieved by immersing the jewelry into an electro-magnetic acid bath which deposits a thin layer of gold, silver, or other metal onto another lesser metal.

EMERALD
Commonly dark-green color, it is also found in varied shades of green. An "emerald-cut" stone is oblong or square-cut since that is the usual cutting for a genuine emerald. Emerald-cut was introduced in the 1920's with the vital interest in Cubism.

ENAMEL
Opaque glass fired to a gloss after it is applied to metal. The metal is dipped into molten colored glass, *without* the wire dividers known as *cloisons*. Enamel work cannot be applied to a *base* metal. It can only be worked on gold or silver.

ENGRAVING
Cutting lines into metal which are either decorative or symbolic. Method used in monogramming a crest, *cartouche*, or escutcheon.

ESCUTCHEON, -ĕs-kŭch-ŭn
Small metal plate used atop an ornament or ring for monogram or signet.

FACET(s)
Small flat surfaces cut into a stone, glass, or shell. Purpose is to refract light or enhance design.

FESTOON
A garland of chain or chains decorated with ornamental drops or pendants which lay on a curve against woman's upper bosom, or drapes across a man's chest. A *chatelaine* chain could well be worn in "festoon fashion", meaning it would be draped from shoulder to shoulder, forming a curve at the center fall.

FILIGREE
To apply thread-like wire and decorate into a lace or cobweb network.

FINDINGS
Metal parts used by jewelers for finishing an ornament.

FLEUR-de-LIS, - flûr'-dĕ-lē'
This was the trade-mark for the city of Verdun, France. The word means "flower of light". The *fleur-de-lis* is the French symbol of life and power, and is designed from nature's Iris. This symbol is found on many Victorian, Edwardian, and *Art Nouveau* pieces and has been carried out in modern designs as well.

FOBS
The terms "fobs" and "charms" were interchangeable from mid-1850 through the 1930's.

Watch fobs or watch charms were in vogue in the 1890's through the turn-of-the-century and certainly on into the '30's when the pocket watch became more popular than ever. They were very desirable in agate, hematite, tiger eye, lava stone, convex crystal, goldstone, inlaid onyx or assorted onyx.

Emblem charms or fobs were made in hard enamel colors with raised emblems. The hard enamel colors represented the particular Orders: Knights of Pythias, Masonic, Oddfellows, Encampment, Eastern Star, etc.

Emblem charms were more intricately produced and wrought in solid gold examples. Solid gold was very heavily engraved with a great deal of raised work and exquisite enameling. The gold work was often incorporated with white or black onyx.

The craftsmanship required for emblem charms and fobs with their raised centers and edges, colored enamels, insets of precious gems and so forth, shows the marvelous skill of the early jewelers.

The same designs used on emblem charms and fobs were utilized for lapel buttons with screw-backs, and required a great deal of finesse in completing the design in miniature.

Ceramic charms and fobs set with bloodstone or agate seals with richly carved slides were hung from the very finest of black silk or human hair finely woven into fob-chains.

FOIL
Silver, gold, or other color thin leaf of metal, used to back imitation gemstones or faceted glass to improve color and provide greater brilliance.

FRENCH ELECTRIC JEWELRY
In 1875, master jewelers in France fashioned a unique and finely wrought piece of jewelry. The design cleverly concealed a thin wire in either vest pocket (men) or hidden down the back of the dress or under hairdo (women). Electric impulses from a battery animated the object, such as moving the eyes, opening the mouth, fluttering the wings, etc. A truly novel conceit utilized in a stickpin for an ascot, or ornament for an *aigrette*.

FRENCH IVORY (also see CELLULOID)
An imitation of ivory tusk in grained Celluloid or plastic. "French Ivory" is a registered trade-mark. Other ivory imitations, not quite as good, were *Ivorette*, *Ivorine*, *Ivory Pyralin*, and *DuBarry Pyralin*. In the 1870's, there was a shortage of ivory for billiard balls and a $10,000 prize was offered for anyone who could

produce a substitute. John Wesley Hyatt mixed nitric acid and cellulose to make *Celluloid*. It was the first plastic to look like ivory. *French Ivory* products were also produced by J.B. Ash Co. of Rockford, Illinois. Since Celluloid was highly flammable, it was eventually replaced by the use of Bakelite and other fire-retardant plastics.

FRENCH JET

This is imitation black glass. The name "French" is a misnomer since most of the so-called "French jet" is actually from Bohemia (Czech.). It is a term which takes in almost all jet and black onyx, other than that which is genuine.

FRENCH PASTE

It was French paste that surpassed that of other countries and the periods of Louis XV and and XVI have been noted as "The Golden Age of Paste". It was worn by the aristocracy, not so much as an *imitation*, but as a *substitute* for the true gems.

Some paste stones notably rhinestones, are set with bright polished foil, a thin leaf of metal placed in back of a gemstone or glass to heighten the brilliance or the color. It is sometimes difficult, unless one is an expert, to distinguish between diamonds, spinels, or French paste. Paste, itself, is a composition of pounded rock-crystal melted with alkaline salts, and colored with metallic oxides, and used primarily for making imitation gems.

GEMS/GEMSTONES

Genuine gems and gemstones are created by natural mysterious forces.

Traditionally, some stones are considered precious and others semi-precious. Diamonds, rubies, sapphires, and emeralds were of the precious variety; all others were considered semi-precious. The more *modern* view is that *all* gems and gemstones are "precious" according to one's individual taste or preference. Therefore, the terms preferred today for classifying all natural stones are gems and/or gemstones. Diamonds, rubies, sapphires, and emeralds are considered gems and all others gemstones.

When relating facets to gems and gemstones the top of the stone is called the *table;* the bottom of the stone is called the *pavillion;* the point or the center is known as the *culet.*

For many centuries past, jewels were considered medicinal. It was believed that some, if not all, precious stones possessed unquestioned healing power. Hebrew tradition states that the Tablets of Moses were of sapphire, and the Hebrew word *"sappir"* means "the most beautiful". It symbolizes loyalty, justice, beauty, and nobility.

St. John writes of the emerald in his Apocalypse. Emeralds from India, Persia, and Peru are the most valuable, and are shown as the emblem of charity, hope, joy, and abundance. It also has the reputation of curing epilepsy and being an all-around pain-killer.

The diamond has always been regarded as the most precious stone. It was believed that if a guilty person wore a diamond it turned red, but in the presence of innocence it would retain its original purity and brilliance. The diamond was reputed to be a preserver against epidemics and poisons, that it calmed anger and formented conjugal love. The ancients called it "the stone of reconciliation". It symbolizes constancy, strength, and innocence.

In ancient times, the opal was considered a splendid stone but due to the belief that it attracted misfortune, it had the effect of lowering the desirability of the stone except for those who were born in October. This, of course, was a mere superstition which seemed to have been founded on a Russian legend which had come into France. It was reported that the Empress Eugenie had a horror of the opal and at the sight of one in the Tuilleries, she was actually terrorized.

The language of gems, their significance, the superstitions connected with gems and gemstones have been written in great depth in many books on stones and lapidary work. In fact, whole volumes have been written about the curiosity of gems, gems as talismans, and so forth. The reader is urged to satisfy his curiosity by searching out the volumes listed in the Bibliography. It is a most fascinating subject and a different aspect of jewelry which should entice the reader into further search.

It is always fashionable, among lovers and friends, to notice the significance attached to the various gems and gemstones and make a pointed effort to give these for birthdays, engagement, and wedding presents.

Birthstones

JANUARY-Garnet. Insures constancy, true friendship and fidelity.
FEBRUARY-Amethyst or Pearl. Freedom from passion and from care.
MARCH-Bloodstone or Hyacinth. Courage, wisdom, and firmness in affection.
APRIL-Diamond. Emblem of innocence and purity.
MAY-Emerald. Discovers false friends and insures true love.
JUNE-Agate or Cat's Eye. Insures long life, health and prosperity.
JULY-Coral or Ruby. Discovers poison, corrects evils resulting from mistaken friendship.
AUGUST-Sardonyx or Moonstone. Without it, no conjugal felicity so must live unloved and alone.
SEPTEMBER-Chrysolite or Sapphire. Frees from evil passions and sadness of the mind.
OCTOBER-Opal. Denotes hope and sharpens the sight and faith of the possessor.
NOVEMBER-Topaz. Fidelity and and friendship. Prevents bad dreams.
DECEMBER-Turquoise. Success and prosperity in love.

This is the language of gems and gemstones.

GERMAN SILVER

Metal which has no actual silver content but is an alloy of copper, zinc, and nickel, with the highest content of nickel to give it a silvery-white color. It is a common base for plating. Also called "nickel silver", "French grey", or "gun metal".

GILT (or GILDED)

A process for plating a die-stamped or hand-wrought piece of base metal to give it a gold or silver color. The gilding is inferior to rolled plate or electroplating.

GOLD (also see CARAT)

Precious metal ore containing alloys which vary depending on desired color and hardness.

Gold colors range from green to dull yellow, to bright pink and even red. White color (color of platinum or silver) is achieved by alloying nickel and a small percentage of platinum to gold; thus, *White Gold* is an alloy of gold with silver, palladium, platinum, or nickel.

Platinum is more a 20th Century metal and is hardly represented in Victorian jewelry.

Gold is twice as heavy as silver, which is perhaps the reason why a more *solid* silver was used while gold was plated, filled, or rolled with inferior alloys. Platinum is even heavier than gold which explains why it was not used for early *baroque* pieces.

The term *carat or karat* is for the fineness of gold. Example: 18K or 750 = 18/24 or 750/1000th which represents 75% pure gold content.

GOLD-FILLED

Joining a layer or layers of gold alloy to a base metal alloy, then rolling or drawing as required for thickness of material.

GOLDSTONE

Adventurine gemstone sparkling with particles of gold-colored minerals; or, man-made brown glass with specks of copper infused within.

GRANULAR WORK

Gold or silver metal applied in decorative designs which resemble tiny grains or pin-heads, roundly shaped.

GYPSY SETTING (also known as BEZEL)

Where top of stone is exposed just above the metal casing.

HAIR ORNAMENTS (also see COMBS and BARRETT)

Hair ornaments were worn from 1850 through the 1910 era. They were executed in high *baroque* style in both gold and sterling silver. Most of the metal was cut, pierced, or engraved, with some fine *repousse'* work.

The *teeth* on both the gold and sterling hair ornaments were either of the same metal as the top ornament or the teeth were inlaid into ivory, bone, and tortoise. Later, there were synthetics such as Celluloid.

In 1893, 14 karat Roman gold hair ornaments were beginning to become popular. They were made with the finest Celluloid teeth, although the heads of the hair ornaments were of solid gold set with gems and gemstones. Hair ornaments ordinarily have a *pair* of teeth whereas combs, which often were made in the same styling, had as many as four to nine teeth, depending on the size of the comb.

HAIR PINS

The *Tortoise Brand* trade-mark was that of Rice & Hochster Makers, New York, and sold for 25¢ per dozen boxes. They were made in three shapes: straight, loop, and crimped, being available in three colors: shell, amber, and black.

The Gibson Girl hairdo at the height of its popularity, required many hair pins in order to keep the *coiffure* neat and in place. This hair style required a great deal of not only one's *natural* hair but additional tresses to give it fullness and beauty. To keep the extra hair pieces, hair switches, and wigs in place, it was necessary to use many hair pins plus two or three combs.

Hair pins were made of rolled gold decorated with birds, butterflies, and stars and these were worn in great profusion throughout the headdress.

In 1921, Swartchild & Co., Chicago, advertised in their catalogue: "The Neverslip Hairpin" for holding eyeglass-chain securely in the hair. The chain extended from the end curve of the hair pin to the small loop at the side of the spectacles or eye glasses.

HALLMARK

An official mark first adopted in England which is incised, punched, or stamped on gold or silver to show quality and to signify purity of metal according to "sterling" or "carat" standard. Other countries' hallmarks indicate origin, patent, manufacture, etc. Unmarked pieces of jewelry are usually American-made since European makers hallmarked theirs. A good way to date American-made jewelry, if it is marked with a patent number, is to note that before 1870 patent numbers reached up to 116000, and after the turn-of-the-century, 694000.

Hallmarks were originally called "trade-marks" which are as old as the industry itself. Ancient Babylon had property symbols, and the Chinese claim to have had trade-marks 1,000 years before Christ. Roman silver was marked with stamps in Byzantine times (7th Century), while the monasteries inspected their plate periodically and applied stamps as a mark of control.

The trade-mark is the development of the familiar shop sign which the Roman invasion introduced into England. In the ruins of Pompeii, discoveries were reported of representations of various kinds of industry such as signs at open doors. A goat meant a dairy. A mule driving a mill was posted at the baker's door. Because of the limited number of trades at the time, signs were employed as we now use street numbers. But as competition increased and many new shops came into being, the street numbers designated the address and the signboard fell into disuse. It was then that the trade-mark became accepted, whereupon the shopkeeper merely placed his mark on the article of merchandise.

Most of the countries in Europe stamped their gold and silver wares with the stiffest control by the Guilds or Goldsmiths' Halls (England), and were called "hallmarks". As early as 1363, England had already passed laws saying that every master goldsmith shall have a *"quote by himself"* and the same mark *"shall be known by them which shall be assigned by the King to survey their work allay"*. That meant that all of the goldsmiths work had to be assayed before they could be put to the mark which was ordained by the King. Such mark would certify the ore content of both the silver and the gold.

By 1857, the word *Sterling* became universally used except here in the United States. Until 1894, no State protection was given to purchases of either gold or silver, and the buyer could only trust the reputation of the maker and dealer.

State laws regulating the stamping of the words *Sterling, Sterling Silver, Coin,* or *Coin Silver,* on wares of silver or metals purporting to be silver, were first passed in 1894, Massachusetts being the leader in this regard; but many other States followed suit within the next ten years. These laws were similar within each State and they specified that any wares which were marked *Sterling* or *Sterling Silver* must contain 925 parts of fine silver in every 1,000 parts. - *Coin* or *Coin Silver*, must contain 900 parts of fine silver in every 1,000. Persons were subject to misdemeanor charges if they attempted to sell merchandise that was marked *Sterling* or *Coin Silver* that did not contain the above-mentioned quantities of pure silver.

Regarding the hallmarking of gold, it had become law that no article was to be offered for sale that did not plainly stamp the exact number of twenty-fourth parts of pure gold or portion of gold that the said article contained. Any person found guilty of violation of the provisions of this act could be fined up to $1,000 or imprisoned in a "common jail" not to exceed one year, or both, "at the discretion of the court".

Hallmarking became so strict that even portions of a particular piece of jewelry had to be marked. For instance, the front of a pin could be marked *Sterling* and the back could be an alloy and it would have to be stamped thus: *sterling front.*

Trade-marks should not be confused with hallmarks inasmuch as a trade-mark is the name of the manufacturing company or the artisan whereas a hallmark is a guarantee of the quality of the ore contained in the merchandise.

HATPIN

A hatpin was used to securely fasten a hat to the hair and head of the wearer. Hatpins measuring from 4" to 12" in length were worn from approximately 1850 to 1920.

It's interesting to note that in some of the early 1890 catalogues, there were two classifications for pins: 1. to secure a bonnet; 2. to secure a hat. One was a *hatpin* and the other was a *bonnet pin.* It's difficult to distinguish one from the other except that the bonnet pin seems to be a bit smaller and the design of the ornament is more of the Victorian Age--somewhat *baroque*, perhaps with a starburst, a flower or a scabbard. The bonnet pins were made of gold plate or of a gold color such as the hair ornaments, whereas many hatpins were featured in sterling silver.

Hatpins were a bit more daring in that they had bow-knots, insects, designs inspired by shells and flowers and there was a great deal of open work departing from the *baroque*-type of *repoussse* which is so often found in hair ornaments and on the bonnet pins. Perhaps the advertisements for *both* bonnet pins and hatpins were to please some 1890 women who refrained from wearing the "masculine" hat, since most women still referred to head coverings as "bonnets". More traditional women preferred calling a hat a bonnet even when there were no longer strings tied under the chin but hung loosely at the sides and were called "lappets".

By 1900, *bonnets* was no longer a term used in magazines published for women. The *"Delineator"* of 1900 thus reported: *"Every woman of intelligence and good taste is aware that her hat either adds to or completely destroys the beauty of her toilette . . ."*

Little toques and turbans were given every type of artifice to make them more attractive, such as plumes, quills, flowers, and rosettes of taffeta or chiffon, each adding to the basic hat a fashionable jet buckle or other type of hat ornament. Small *toques* were hats which set atop the Gibson Girl hairdo and were "speared and settled" by equally luxurious hatpins which oftentimes matched

132

the buckles, hat and dress ornaments. To each millinery creation a note of brilliancy was added by the rhinestone buckle, the jeweled ornament, and the several fashionable hatpins which had reached the height of popularity in 1900-1913.

In December 1910, there was an article in *"The Five and Ten Cent Magazine"*, which stated that 1910 was *"the greatest season for big hatpins in the history of the trade"*. Hatpins were large enough to hold powder puffs, mirrors, trinkets, and small change. They were being shown for the Christmas trade by the manufacturing jewelers. Guards were used to cover the dangerous points of the pins.

J.A. & S.W. Granberry, (Newark, N.J.), manufactured 10-carat hatpins which were trade-marked with a "G" in a diamond. The head of the ornament was marked accordingly but the pins were steel stems and therefore not hallmarked. Theodore W. Foster & Bros. Co., was established in 1873 at Providence, R.I., and manufactured rolled and gold-filled hatpins. Day, Clark & Co. were makers of fine jewelry in 14-carat only. Their manufacturing company was located in Newark, N.J., and they turned out hatpins in *"modish styles and lengths"*. Potter, Symbol & Buffington Co., (Providence, R.I.), produced gold hatpins, whereas Henry W. Fishel and Sons, Inc., (New York), manufactured sterling hatpins with their trade-mark "F & Co." in a horizontal diamond.

"If you are riding in a car in New York or vicinity and you observe a vision in blue or pink draw forth her twelve-inch hatpin and deftly unfasten the end, don't be afraid that she is going to come close to gouging out your eye or tear away a large section of your face. Watch her closely, and from the head of that pin you will see her draw forth a rouge rag or possibly a powder puff and a small, circular mirror. A few strokes on the cheek, several peeks into the small circular glass will then follow, and then the pin will be returned to the hat . . . the new fad has caught on in New York with a vengeance. Department stores and other shops are doing a land-office business". (From *"The Five and Ten Cent Magazine,"* 1910.)

The author has written the first definitive work on the subject of hatpins titled *"The Collector's Encyclopedia of Hatpins and Hatpin Holders"*, published by Collector Books. For those interested in pursuing the subject of hatpins in depth, the author suggests her aforementioned work published in 1976.

HEMATITE, -hĕm'-a-tīt

A blood-like red iron ore which in the form of cyrstals is used primarily as settings for men's jewelry. Brown hematite, called limonite in modern-day usage, refers to either the reddish-brown or the brown color.

ILLUSION SETTING

A setting in which the stone is made to appear larger by cutting metal in shape of gem-table.

IMITATION (also see SYNTHETICS)

To make out of other materials a substance resembling the natural element, i.e., paste or rhinestones for gems; hard rubber, dyed and then molded into coral-color flowers; plastic tortoise shell; "French Ivory" which is an imitation of ivory, bone, etc. Imitation is not the same as synthetic.

INTAGLIO, -in-tăl'-yō

To cut a design deeply on the obverse or front of a gem or other type material. Intaglio is the opposite of *repousse* in that *repousse* work is a method of incising from the reverse side or back of a metallic object.

IRIDESCENT
To give a high luster to pearls, glass, or other material.

JADE
A hard stone with a resinous or oily aspect when polished. Jade is not actually carved but is cut or chipped, chiseled, or ground into the desired size and shape, then polished. Jade is found in many shades, and the presence of quantities of iron determines the color. The colors vary: mutton fat (sometimes streaked with gray or brown tones); green (spinach or moss colors); celadon (off-white color); tangerine; pink; lavender; and the most desirable color, luminous apple-green called Imperial Jade.

Jade is formed into amulets, hair ornaments, rings, bracelets, beads, necklaces, pendants, and Chinese burial pieces called "weights" for the tongue and eyes.

Because jade is a tough, hard, resilient stone, it cannot be easily scratched, whereas imitation jade (called by many new names) can scratch. One of the most common imitations of jade is dyed calcite which is nothing more than ordinary marble, chalk or limestone.

One of the finest collections of both Oriental and Burmese Jade in America is exhibited in the private Jade Room at Gumps Department Store, San Francisco.

Although jade occurs in Asia, America, and other countries, the Oriental jade is most desirable.

Nephrite jade is found on mainland China, jadeite is from Burma, and there is an American jade which is found in Wyoming.

JARGOW-NIB
A 1913 nickname for hatpin point "protectors", named for Berlin Police President, von Jargold, who sought to enforce the wearing of hatpin safeties by law.

JET (GENUINE and IMITATION)
Jet is the name given most black jewelry whether it be genuine or glass. Genuine jet will retain its sparkling polish for many years while "black glass" (also known as "French Jet", even though most glass came from Bohemia), will crack, scratch, and become dull.

Genuine jet is a brown-black lignite in which the texture or grain of the original fossilized wood of which this particular coal is comprised, can still be seen. It can be brought to a high polish and is thus easily imitated in glass. The finest genuine jet comes from Whitby (England) where over 200 workshops produced Victorian Era jewelry. Jet was associated purely with mourning, although it had been worn in earlier times as decorative jewelry. Jet jewelry was considered proper wear during the first year of mourning, then diamonds or pearls were allowable during the second period of mourning. During those first two years, a widow was expected to wear "widow's weeds" and at that time, no earrings were worn in the street. This was etiquette, circa 1850 - 1900.

JEWELERS (1850-1950)

For biographical sketches about note-worthy jewelers and manufacturing firms (1850-1950), refer to two excellent sources listed below:

"*Modern Jewelry*", by Graham Hughes, and

"*Victorian Jewelry Design*", by Charlotte Gere.

Both are listed in the Bibliography.

Familiar trade-marks on jewelry sold in most American department stores and jewelry shops:

Coro and *Trifari* - (both estab. late 1800's). *Trifari* is the trade-mark for Trifari Krussman and Fishel, Inc., East Providence, R.I.; Coro, Inc., is in Providence.

Monet and *Weiss* are also represented in fine jewelry departments.

Emmons, Caroline Emmons Div., C.H. Stuart and Company, Inc., Newark, New York State, initiated "*jewelry home fashion shows*" in 1949, and did much to bring finer costume jewelry out of the "dime store trade", into high-fashion. Emmon's sister company, "Sarah Coventry", offered fashion costume jewelry at lower cost.

For information about American jewelers, write to *Jewelers Board of Trade*, Providence, Rhode Island.

Types of Jewelry Design and Countries
Predominant in Producing Jewelry
1850 - 1950

Period	Design	Country
1850-1895	Greek & Etruscan "Sporting" Jewelry Victorian Baroque, Gothic & Renaissance	Bohemia England France Germany Italy
1885-1910	*Art Nouveau* Egyptian Oriental Victorian Period Renaissance	America Bohemia Denmark England France Germany Italy
1910-1950	*Art Deco* *Art Moderne* *Modern*	All of Above plus American Indian Asian Countries Israel Mexico South America

Material for Jewelry and Jeweled Accessories
(1850 - 1950)

Ores--Metals	Natural Elements	Man-Made
Aluminum	Amber	*Bakelite*
Brass	Bog Oak	*Celluloid*
Bronze	Bone	Glass (Rhinestone)
Chrome	Cinnabar	Paste (French & Strass)
Copper	Coral	*Plastics* (French Ivory, etc.)
Gold	Gems & Gemstones	
Iron	Hair	Porcelain
Pewter	Horn	
Pinchbeck	Ivory	
Palladium	Jade	
Platinum	Jet	
Rhodium	Marcasite	
Silver	Pearl	
Steel	Sea Shell	
	Stone (Mosaics)	
	Tortoise Shell	
	Tooth	
	Tusk	
	Wood	

Italics: Primarily 20th Century jewelry

LAPIS LAZULI, - lăp'-ĭs lăz-u-lī
Deep blue sometimes containing gold-colored specks of iron pyrites. Horn stone or jasper is sometimes artificially colored to represent Lapis gems.

LAVALIERE, - lăv'-à-lēr' (also LAVALIERE/LAVALLIERE)
Named for the Duchess de La Valliere (1644-1710), mistress of Louis XIV, this type of jewelry is an ornament hanging from a chain which is worn around the neck. The terms *"lavaliere"* and "pendant" could be used interchangeably. However, the term *"lavaliere"* does not appear on jewelers' catalogues until after 1900.

Pendants and *lavalieres* both have small jump rings or fancy type loops into which a chain is threaded. Pendants, before the turn-of-the-century, had a heavy *baroque* type of drop, whereas those from the 1910-1913 periods represent the more beautiful *lavalieres* of the *Art Nouveau* Period with delicate open work, scroll-work, and intricate filigree set with very small half-pearls, opals, garnets, etc. The high period for *lavalieres* was 1910-1920.

LOCK (JEWELRY BOX or JEWELRY CASKET)
Jewel boxes or jewelry caskets are profusely illustrated in many of the catalogues before the turn-of-the-century. They usually came equipped with locks and keys which were little gems of the jeweler's art. They had gold or silver fronts and the shapes and engraving are delightful to behold. Unfortunately, most have gone by the wayside and it is rare to find these beautiful Victorian jeweled locks with their complimentary keys.

Jewelry boxes, cases, and caskets with locks and keys were sold separately and were advertised in catalogues from 1893 through 1915.

LOCKETS

These ornaments hung from neck chains and bracelets, and were worn as charms or fobs. They were designed in ovals, rounds, hearts, and other varied shapes. Lockets opened to hold one, two, and often three or more photographs, as well as mementoes such as pressed flowers or a lock of hair. They were embossed, chased, engraved, enameled; many were set with gems and gemstones or had pictorial or floral scenes in *repousse*.

Lockets were made of gold, silver, rolled gold and plate. The gold-front lockets for gentlemen, which were worn with their waist or vest chains, were larger and much more intricately worked and designed than other type lockets. The solid gold front of the locket called for high relief and design work and many were set with rubies and sapphires which accentuated a scenic engraving. The chased frames and edges of the lockets were finished with lovely chasing.

By 1893, the new platinum was being introduced into more and more jewelry but the overwhelmingly popular metal for lockets was Roman yellow and gold with platinum still a rare commodity. The *intaglio* cameo was a very desirable design on the gold-front lockets and many of them were set with tiger eye, onyx, or genuine brown sard.

The locket from 1890 through WWI was probably the most sentimental gift for men, women, and children. To this day, it still remains a highly prized piece of jewelry.

LORGNETTE, - lôr-nyĕt'

A *lorgnette* is a pair of eye-glasses or an opera glass which is attached to a handle. A *lorgnon* is actually a single glass such as a monocle, but ordinarily speaking the *lorgnon* could be substituted for *lorgnette.*

Most *lorgnons* close like eye-glasses; there were tiny ones that were made for *chatelaines*, and some that were so small they were called "glove *lorgnons*".

Frames could be from simple to luxurious items. Some of these were jewel encrusted, or encased in tortoise-shell or mother-of-pearl and some had a crest engraved in gold. Shell and horn were best sellers and were made by European craftsmen.

There were wrist chains used especially for the glove *lorgnon*. Chains and *lorgnons* frequently go together and the same decorative treatement was usually applied to both. In 1880 *lorgnettes* made of zylonite (plastic) were offered for sale. Zylonite was also used for opera glass holders (a type of *lorgnette*).

The *Art Nouveau* Period produced exquisite *lorgnettes*. Lorgnettes could fold in half on a small hinge and slide into the handle of the *lorgnette*. The flowing *Art Nouveau* lines lent itself to this article and many of the *lorgnette* frames were jewel encrusted with curved handles that represented twisted stems of flowers or women with flowing hair.

Lorgnette chains were set with pearls, turquoise, rubies, opals, diamonds, and imitation gems and gemstones. A swivel was at the end of the chains to which spectacles, fans, or eye-glasses could be attached. Other type chains had a pin clasp for fastening to the clothing. The demise of the *lorgnette* came with the Great Depression of the 1930's when theaters and other places of luxury were less frequented and the sobering events dictated a less "affected" stance by high society in face of mass poverty.

MARCASITE

A white iron pyrite; if the ore is yellow, it takes on the appearance of "fool's gold". Cut steel jewelry and marcasites resemble one another in color and in faceted treatment, but cut steel will rust easily and is not as hard nor as brilliant as marcasites. Most marcasite jewelry is made in France.

MARQUISE CUT, - mar-kēz'

Popular cut for diamonds in which the stone is brilliantly faceted and then shaped like an elongated almond or tear-drop.

MATCH SAFE

This term is an early expression still familiar just prior to the turn-of-the-century. The match safe was small compared to the larger version which came after 1905 and was then called "match boxes" which were made in either gold, silver, or plated base metals.

MEDALS and BADGES

Given for prizes and testimonials, they came in many shapes and designs. There were medals for rowing, tennis, baseball, gun club, bicycle, shooting, bowling, and athletics. It is noted in various catalogues printed after 1900, that to the previous awards were added: scholarship, music, good conduct, society, special prize, prize essay, and art.

Most medals and badges were intricately engraved and enameled, many with escutcheons carrying the Heraldic Crest or a monogram of the donor. The recipient's name, date, and the occasion was engraved on the reverse side of the medals and badges.

Medals could be worn from a chain, whereas badges were more often associated with the type that was pinned to a lapel, shirtwaist, or uniform. Badges were often sewn on various color ribbons, measuring from ½" to 3" in length. Fastening pins with clasps were then inserted at one end of the ribbon, and the badge hung from there.

MEDALLIONS (see CHARMS or FOBS)

Shaped like a medal, from which it derives its name, but in treatment is more like a highly engraved charm or fob.

MEMORIAL JEWELRY (see MOURNING, MEMENTO, and HAIR JEWELRY)

MILLEFIORI, -mil'e-fi-o-re

Multi-colored mosaic beads requiring great skill of the glassblower to create florals, animals, etc. They are most familiar in paper weights. Glass beads were manufactured in Italy, primarily on the island of Murano which produced highly prized "trade beads".

MINE CUT (or OLD MINE CUT)

Gems from South America, mostly Brazil, before diamond mines were discovered in Africa. The cut differs from "European cut" in that it was thicker from the table to the culet (the bottom facet), and the point (culet) was cut off flat.

MOONSTONE

Transparent but more often translucent gemstone with pearly or opaline luster.

MOSAIC

Creating motif or design parquetry with minute pieces of colored glass or stone which have been set into plaster. Individual portions of the design are sectioned by metal, similar to form used in *cloisonne*. This type of Venetian jewelry work is also called *pietra dura* and was utilized for such designs as foliage, leaves, flowers, pebbles, etc. In *pietra dura* the mosaic design is usually set in dull black, either jet or mosaic stone.

MOTHER-OF-PEARL

Differs from abalone in color in that it is the iridescent inner-shell layer of a pearl oyster.

MOUNTING

The specific adaptation of a stone or artifact within a cage, frame, or setting, usually comprised of metal.

MOURNING JEWELRY

Black jewelry, either real or imitation jet, black onyx, ebony, or bog oak, popularized during Queen Victoria's period of mourning (1861-1901), upon the death of her Prince Consort, Albert.

Onyx and jet were the stones most widely worn for mourning jewelry.

A fine source-book for Victorian symbolism (the language of flowers in mourning jewelry and love brooches) is: *"Victorian Sentimental Jewellery"* listed in the Bibliography.

NECKLACES (see *LA VALIERE*, PENDANTS, CHARMS, BEADS, and other specific types)

NODDER (also called "BOBBLER", "SPRINGER", "TREMBLER", OR "TREMBLANT")

A short spring which caused an ornamental head to bobble or bounce freely. Several short springs or wires could be utilized on a bouquet of metallic flowers set with brilliants which would then sparkle as they moved and caught the light.

OPALESCENCE

A pearly sheen from inside a gem such as a moonstone.

PASTE

A superior glass containing oxide of lead used for jewelry to imitate gems and gemstones. Joseph Strass perfected paste, although paste was used since ancient times as imitations of precious stones. French paste is considered superior to all others. Even today there are jewelry designers using paste which appeals to the "Jet Set" who are fearful of wearing their real gems in public. However, in Victorian and Edwardian times, much of the French paste jewelry was not so much an *imitation* of jewels as a *substitution*.

Most paste is actually a composition of pounded rock-crystal melted with alkaline salts, and colored with metallic oxides.

PARURE, -pà-roor'

Matching jewelry containing several pieces such as necklace, choker, brooch, earrings, bracelet, and ring. Demi-*parure* consists of only two to three matching pieces.

PAVE SETTING, -pá-vá'
Stones placed so closely together that almost no metal shows between them.

PEACOCK EYE
A glass whose coloring resembles the "eye" of a peacock feather.

PEARLS (also see WAX BEAD PEARL)
Pearls are the natural formation of a secretion called nacre within an oyster caused by some irritating substance such as a grain of sand. When the pearls are naturally formed they are called *Oriental*. Cultured pearls are made by nature with the help of man. This man-induced process originated and was patented by Kokichi Mikimoto, 1896. Nacre, an iridescent shell-like substance, coats the natural or man-induced irritant which forms a pearl.

Cultured and Oriental pearls both come from the oyster; however, there are fake pearls made with fish scales as well as glass beads covered by an iridescent wax-like coating called wax-bead pearls which originally came from Italy and Bohemia. The latter type will eventually turn into a dullish beige color whereas the Cultured or natural Oriental pearl will retain its high luster.

Some pearls are formed in perfect rounds, other acquire a "blister" or *baroque* shape. Strings of perfectly matched round pearls are most valuable.

Fresh-water pearls are called "river pearls". Salt-water pearls are primarily mounted in 18-carat gold and platinum, while freshwater or river pearls are set in lower carat.

1915-1916 was the year that the odd-shaped iridescent pearl was in demand and most came from Italy's Murano Island where artificial pearls were nothing more than glass covered by a paste made of fish scales.

Pearls are thought of as mere off-white iridescent colors but they are found in variations of pink, grays, and black, the latter pearl so highly prized.

PEKING GLASS
When it is a light green glass, it is sometimes called "poor man's jade" however, it is manufactured in many other shades of glass, imitating the colors of jade that are available.

PENDANTS (also see *LA VALIERE* and MEDALLIONS)
In 1910 the vogue for low collars invited all sorts of pretty neck ornaments such as pendants, medallions, and *lavalieres,* as well as brooches. The most favored at that time was the pendant, which was often enhanced by black *moire* ribbon rather than a chain.

The delicate metal work was invariably either the cool gray of platinum which was coming into prolonged use, silver or French metal. Many of the beautiful *lavalieres* or pendants included fine wires twisted as in filigree work, and much of the metal had a very thin edge or depth. Enamel work was very popular then and jewelry as a whole became much less *baroque* than in Victorian times.

PENCILS
During the 1890-1920 period there were gold and fine rolled plate pencils which were highly featured in many of the jewelers' catalogues. This is particularly true of the collapsible pencils which were made with silver chasing, enameling, with many having a white Celluloid barrel that resembled ivory. Others had a fluted finish, a swirl pattern, or a nobby rustic finish which resembled a piece of bamboo. Some pencils were worn on a chain but the long, thin *grosgrain* ribbon with fancy engraved slides were highly featured.

PHOTO JEWELRY

Photo jewelry came in right after the turn-of-the-century. In fact, the Cranley Photo Button Mfg. Co. of Chicago advertised in 1901: "...*any picture you mail us reproduced on*...*two, handsome cuff buttons and four shirtwaist studs*...*complete for $1.00. We also make scarf pins, hatpins, watch charms, brooches, belt buckles, and medallions*". The company assured the purchaser that the pictures would be returned "uninjured".

Photo jewelry became very popular with the rush of improvements in photography. There was a photo button which was actually *pinned* on rather than sewn. This was called a Photo Miniature and cost ten cents from the Bullard Button Co. of Kansas City, Missouri. The ten cents, by the way, was to "*cover the cost of reproduction, packing, and the postage*". The advertisement showed a beautiful gold braided brooch into which the photograph was bezel set. This brooch was offered free providing that the customer would get them additional business. Again, as in most advertisements, the agents for companies were paid in premiums, primarily jewelry, in exchange for their sales work.

PIERCE WORK

Die-cast frame which is cut and engraved with a great deal of open work in the metal.

PIETRA DURA, -pyā'trä dōō'rä

The art of using colored mosaic *stone* highly treasured in Victorian times, which more recently is represented by *glass* mosaics. The Florentine *pietra dura* examples are of cut stone, coral and malachite. They usually were comprised of a floral pattern which was then adhered to black marble. *Pietra dura*, as with other mosaics, was produced in the early half of the 19th Century. Today we are beginning to receive some fine examples of mosaic work from Italy after a long period when this type of jewelry was lacking in the marketplace.

PINCHBECK

A name used for the manufacture of imitation gold jewelry, sometimes called "pom pom". Pinchbeck got its name from Christopher Pinchbeck, a London clockmaker who in 1732 introduced 15% zinc into brass in a special process which resembled gold. The process for pinchbeck "gold" was buried with the demise of its maker, Christopher Pinchbeck; however, with the introduction of electroplating, it's likely pinchbeck would have gone that route anyway.

PINS (BLOUSE/WAIST/NECK-PINS/"BEAUTY PINS"/VEIL PINS/etc. Also see BROOCHES)

Because yesteryear lacked today's modern laundry conveniences, collars, cuffs, frills, ribbons, etc., were detachable. Many of the collars and cuffs, etc., were *pinned* in place by exquisite "lace pins" which were most often of delicate filigree or open work.

Men wore few decorative pins for shirts, except for the cravat or stickpins since their cuffs, shirt backs and fronts, and collars were worn with studs or buttons. There was a pin, however, called a "frill" which was used for men's dress-wear which was a rather elaborate frilled shirt worn before the turn-of-the-century.

A small pin, which has long since been forgotten, was the novelty "safety pin" that came in around 1901. These were offered in 10-carat gold and were sometime scalled "negligee collar pins". They resembled a very narrow barrett or bar pin. They were also called "handy pins", sold in pairs, in a myriad of design, executed in a gold front, gold filled, sterling silver, or black enamel.

The bar pin is actually represented by what its terminology implies: a simple 1" to 2" bar, very narrow, of either gold or silver. The simple bar pin had many, many innovations and variations of the jeweler's art so that in looking at the various catalogues one may find several dozen styles.

Sterling silver brooch pins were most often engraved or had open lacework or filigree work. The *baroque* scroll patterns were the most desirable in the Victorian Era.

Veil pin sets were three various size "bar pins" or "handy pins" which were small, sold in either pairs, three or four on a card, all of which were joined with a chain to prevent loss. Similarly, waist sets also came three pins per set as did negligee collar pins and button pin sets.

Shirtwaist was the name for blouses in America whereas in France they were called *"chemisettes"*. In both instances, they imitated the *Renaissance* sleeve which was a fullness at the cuff and then the cuff was accentuated with some beautiful cuff buttons.

Cuff *pins* were sold in pairs and they were very small and resembled small baby pins or safety pins sold before the turn-of-the-century. The very small pins, some of them no larger than 1/2" long and 1/8" wide, were used as you would employ buttons for children's clothing or for the pre-teenager. They were exquisitely engraved in enamel, very often carrying the words *"Baby"*, *"Pet"*, *"Darling"*, signifying the filial attachment of the family to the newborn. It's very possible that the mortality rate of infants before 1900 was so great that the baby in the Victorian home was considered extremely precious.

Cape or jersey pins could either match or compliment one another since there were two attached to a chain. For instance, one could have a heart at the head of one pin and the other a *fleur-de-lis*. Another pair might have an arrow and a clover. They were made in solid gold, rolled gold plate and in sterling silver. Silver by all counts was never as popular a color metal for jewelry until the *Art Nouveau* Period (1895-1910).

"Beauty pins" were in vogue during the 1901-1910 period. They were worn in place of studs in the front of waists or blouses and came in threes or fours. They were very tiny, measuring no more than ¼" to ½" and were enameled with the most delicate flowers such as tiny violets or forget-me-nots. Most were beautifully enameled and in exquisite detail.

The main difference between pins and brooches is that pins are first *utilitarian* and then decorative, whereas brooches are primarily decorative. Today we refer to all kinds of decorataive brooches as *pins*.

PIQUE , - pē̇-kā̄́

Inlaying of gold and/or silver into genuine tortoise-shell.

PLASTICS (also see BAKELITE and CELLULOID)

Term applied to a group of synthetic chemical products with the distinctive quality which enables them to be molded, carved, laminated, or pressed into many shapes, sizes, and designs. Tortoise, horn, mother-of-pearl, wood, marble, jet, and amber were all imitated in plastics.

Some imitations for natural elements were called, (as in the case of tortoise), *"tortone"*, advertised as "non-breakable" by E. & J. Bass, New York. *"Tortoisene"* was manufactured by Harry Maynard, Washington, D.C., and Wm. K. Potter of Providence, R.I. established his genuine Tortoise Shell Works. Horn and Celluloid were produced by Alfred Burke & Co., Leominster, Mass., and Thomas Long Co. of Boston. Besides "French ivory" being produced, there was also *"ivoire Parisienne"*, which was an imitation ivory.

As with fine French paste, plastic jewelry--particularly of the *Art Deco* Period and the *Art Moderne* pieces of the '30's and '40's-- are not *imitations* but an art form in themselves. Renditions in Bakelite and the finer plastics from 1920-1940 are examples of what exquisite artistry could be accomplished in plastics.

Plastic jewelry was produced in the 1940's because of metal shortages due to World War II.

PLATINUM

From the Spanish work *"platin"*, meaning silver. Most platinum jewelry issued forth primarily after 1920, with the new discoveries of platinum in Canada and South America.

Platinum is much more expensive than gold due to its rarity and because it is heavier than gold, it is not often used in larger jewelry pieces. Rhodium and palladium are of the platinum family, while chrome is an alloy which is utilized for very good, hard, shiny surfaces. Platinum itself, however, is a more dull silver-color, very rich when set with diamonds or other precious gems. Platinum is still a very rare and expensive commodity.

PLIQUE-A -JOUR, - plē-kā'a'jèr'

A translucent *cloisonne* in which there is no metal backing for the enamel work. Rene Lalique was a master craftsman of *plique-a-jour* type enameling.

PURSES (BAGS)

Most collectors may be surprised to learn that mesh bags were works of very fine jewelers. Diamonds and other precious stones were often threaded into the mesh, and the designs were actually outlined in jewels. Some purses were made entirely of seed pearls.

Enamels and precious jewels were set quite lavishly on the frames very rich with *repousse,* hand engraving or cutwork. Gemstones were introduced in the clasp or into the chain. The bags were made as carefully as a jeweler would make a watch and many required no less than three months to complete because of the intricate workmanship.

Jet bags were considered suitable for mourning until the 1920's, then they were also considered quite fashionable when *not* in mourning. Cut steel beads were very popular and bead bags, with conventional floral colors, were considered handsome and dressy. The frame usually matched the tone of the beads used.

Beaded purses were much less expensive than those demanding the very finest in jeweler's art, and they were in fact called beaded bags rather than mesh purses.

Mesh bags were made with fancy weaves such as the star pattern, zig-zag, plaid, daisy pattern, basket weave, herring-bone, and even reversible mesh.

At the beginning of the 20th Century, the mesh purse went to quite the extreme using pinks and greens, or purples and blue ostrich feathers dyed and then sewn right onto the purses. They were really much more daring and less conservative than the previous mesh and beaded bags that were shaped more like valances and were square except that the *new* purses were of the *triangular* shape, so that the coins would drop dead-center into the "point" and not get lost.

"Opera and handkerchief bags" were in vogue during the autumn season, October 1901. They were reported to be delicately tinted suede embroidered in mock gems.

The frames, clasps, and chains for the purses or bags were usually of gold and were purchased separately; the bag itself being made at the home by the ladies who were particularly gifted in "parlor work" or home handicrafts.

Into the handkerchief bag went small vanities such as a pencil and memorandum book, as well as a delicately enameled pair of opera glasses.

Many of the women's magazines had directions for making the various types of pouches which were then attached to the jeweled frames to complete the purse or bag.

Unless marked *sterling*, silver mesh purses were mainly of German silver or gun metal. Silver mesh purses were designed either with a drawstring, a bracelet loop, or with a finely detailed snap-type frame which were done with high relief work or set with imitation stones. Sterling mesh bags were manufactured by Weizenegger Bros., Newark, N.J., while Levitt & Gold, New York, made 14-karat and platinum mesh bags. Another famous American maker was Whiting-Davis.

Beaded *drawstring* bags were highly fashionable accessories in the "jazz age" of the *Roarin' Twenties.* Many of these beaded drawstrings were imported from France and were of sterling or had gold frames set with precious stones.

Beaded bags, unlike those made of silk threads, cording, yarn, etc., faded but beads always kept their beautiful, original color. Most beads were iridescent with high luster and were transparent. Silk thread being opaque, absorbed the color of the bead and the thread and the beads blended. In other words, purple beads combined with a violet thread, light and medium blue beads with a gray or other shades of blue thread, etc.

Bead makers described their wares as " . . .*gold iridescent lusters and transparent iridescent beads. Radiant shades, such as golden brown, jade green, violet, etc., are blended with tints of translucent gold in the same beads to make truly gorgeous bags . . .*"

REPOUSSE, re̱-po͞o-sā'
Decorating metal by pushing out from behind or the reverse side in order to create a design in relief.

RHINESTONE
Takes its name but no element from the River Rhine, Germany. It is a faceted glass stone, usually set with foil backing to give it highlights. It is inferior to French paste or *strass* and cannot be cleaned successfully; once the foil backing is scratched or marred, it loses its luster.

RHODIUM
Term normally used when electroplating objects with a platinum alloy.

RIM
The outside edge of a set stone.

RINGS
There's a great deal of sweet romance and legend bound up in the wedding

ring. When the first glow of Christianity lighted the world, Pliny the Elder told of a custom that his people had borrowed from the ancients of the Nile, that of giving a ring of iron to pledge a betrothal. Such customs from the dim past and the ceremonies which thereby developed, definitely changed from those early times though the Victorian times into something resembling the custom of marriage in the mid-'30's and '40's. Weddings became more *fashionable* in character rather than *religious*, and the desirability of more attractive and eye-catching ring-jewelry was at its height.

The "father of jewelry" was Prometheus. According to Pliny, Prometheus was cut loose from the chains which fastened him to Mount Caucasus by Hercules. Prometheus made a ring out of one of the links of chains which bound him, and in that link he bezel-set a portion of the rock against which he had been chained. This was considered the first ring and the first "gem".

In 1839, Prince Albert presented Queen Victoria with a wedding ring in the form of a serpent. Between that presentation and the opening of King Tut's Tomb, the serpent motif is found in just about every form of jewelry form 1839 to the *Art Deco* Period and into the early '30's.

Men's rings had a renewal of interest in the late twenties and thirties due to the influence of matinee idol, Francis X. Bushman.

In 1900 rings with colored stones were not in vogue for engagement rings. The fashionable engagement ring was the one we know today, a solitaire diamond or smaller stones set in a simple mounting.

"Anti-rheumatic" rings came in just before the turn-of-the-century; they were of gold shell on the outside with gray metal on the inside.

In 1901, *"The Delineator"* reported that beautiful rings *"proper for a man"*, would be a solitaire diamond, a ruby, cat's eye, or other precious stone mounted in a gypsy or handsome carved gold setting.

Women did not consider rings their province or jewelry until the early 18th Century. Prior to that, most men of nobility wore rings as seals. The period when rings were most commonly worn by both sexes was from 1875 to 1900. Rings regained popularity around 1910 to the present day.

Double-ring wedding ceremonies were initiated during WWII. "Token rings" were the most desirable gift for the betrothed from 1880 to around 1910. Such a ring was called *"Mizpah"* ring with clasped hands. *Mizpah*, translated means: *"The Lord watch between me and thee, when we are absent one from another"*.

The most frequently worn men's rings 1850-1950 were emblem rings: Masonic, Knights of Pythias, Odd Fellows, Loyal Order of Moose, Modern Woodmen, Knights of Columbus, Red Men, Brotherhood of Trainmen, etc. Women also wore emblem rings: B.P.O.E. associated with the Elks, Eastern Star, etc.

From 1890-1910, initial rings with raised work and set with an onyx were ordered through catalogues as well as signet rings, which were highly engraved. The stones most often implemented in emblem, initial, and signet rings were: garnet, carbuncle, bloodstone, pink and whitestone cameo, sardonyx, moss agate, opals, moonstone, pyrites of iron and pearls.

ROLLED GOLD

A thin leaf of gold used in plating lesser metals. Methods vary from rolling to electroplating a coat of gold over an inferior metal.

ROSE CUT

The faceting of a gem, genuine or imitation, before the turn-of-the-century.

The brilliant-cut was not commonly used before 1905, but by 1920 the brilliant-cut faceting of diamonds and other gemstones in that superior method did away with the ordinary rose-cut of the earlier era.

SAUTOIR, -sō'twär'

A term popularized in 1890 to designate a very long, narrow gold link chain with either a pearl, a diamond, polished agate bead, etc., introduced at 1" or 2" intervals for the length of the chain. In most instances, the *sautoir* fell below the waistline and was held in place at the waist by a brooch. The chain was fastened together by a jeweled slide which prevented its separation at the bosom. Other types flaunted tassels which hung 3" to 6" longer, requiring the chain to be *tucked in* at the waistline.

In the first decade of the 20th Century, *sautoirs* were advertised in various jewelry catalogues as long chains with tassels or with a center drop to accomodate detachable tassels, pendants, or other conceits. The term is now considered archaic, though it is sometimes revived as a term for the extremely long beaded necklaces of the twenties.

Some *sautoirs* are termed as 20" chains with center drop chains measuring 6" to 8" from which ornaments can be hung; also, as long strings of chains or beads or pearls ending with 2" to 4" tassels.

SECESSION, -sē-sésh-ŭn

An "anti-historical" style of *Art Nouveau* jewelry from Bohemia (1900-1920).

SETTING (see specific type)

A means of incorporating gems, gemstones (genuine, synthetic, or imitation), into metal or other element, with designs known as: BEZEL, BOX, CHANNEL, CLAW, GYPSY, CROWN, ILLUSION, METAL CUP (rhinestones), and PAVE'.

SCARF PINS (also see STICKPINS and TIE PINS)

Scarf pins were made for both ladies and gentlemen as seen in the early catalogues (1890-1930). By the 1920's, they were already being called *cravat pins* and *tie pins* for men and *scarf pins* for the ladies.

No distinction was made between male or female styles and were evidently worn by either sex. Many of the pins had a spiral device which kept them from slipping out; others had fancy innovations such as small shafts at the heads which would secure them against slippage or loss.

Others were thrust into the scarf and then the top ornamental pieces actually flipped forward so as to secure them into place.

Scarf pins offer no end to diversity of design and are set with gems, gemstones, imitation stones, and synthetics.

Advertisements for scarf pins most often read: *"set with brilliants"* which usually referred to a glass "diamond" or doublet of a popular gem such as garnet, opal, ruby, moonstone, or turquoise.

SILVER GILT

Silver with a thin coat of gold or yellow lacquer to produce a rich golden color.

SIGNET

A design in a ring or a fob which is sometimes utilized as a seal because of its *intaglio* carving. The design is usually represented by initials, a crest, or something symbolic. The *intaglio* work itself may be in either stone, gem, glass, or metal.

SLEEVE BUTTONS (STUDS)

Sleeve buttons came in pairs and were designed quite differently than cuff links. Most sleeve buttons snapped while some had a leverback, a small bar attached by a chain wire. Sometimes the bar matched the frontpiece of the button and was usually decorated with engraving or scroll-work.

The variety of men's sleeve buttons are endless! They had many which were engraved with insignias that were very large; many had a real *intaglio* cameo design, a cut tiger eye, or *intaglio* seal of a particular Order.

Tiger eye, goldstone, lava stone, exquisite raised work or *repousse*, emblems, intricately raised designs, all were beautifully executed and often set with either a real gem or a polished "brilliant". Oxidized metals were popular and onyx and the hematite were foremost in desirability.

SLIDES

French slides were mass-produced in gold-filled or gilded-metal, *baroque* in design, but depending on raised work and enamels rather than jewels.

English slides relied heavily on inlay work incorporating large pieces of bloodstone, carnelian, and onyx, set into 9 to 18-carat; others of less artistry were of rolled gold and silver.

American slides braved the brilliance of many gemstones set into delicately engraved, tiny slides. Larger slides housed garnets, onyx, cameos, rubies, diamonds, and emeralds, with much Etruscan-style intricacy or granule work.

Slides are to be found in round, flat, square, oblong, oval, barrel-shaped and other metallic improvisations executed in low-carat to 18-carat, gold filled, rolled gold and silver. They range in size from ¼" to 2", with tubular findings to permit passage of a chain. Other designed slides allowed chains to pass through two holes on either side of hollow-work which was cork-filled to prevent slippage.

Slides have become collectible for handsome bracelets. Be alert to the fine *copies* of slides which are in the marketplace as well as very cheap reproductions.

SPECTACLES PIN-HOLDER (EYE-GLASS HOLDER)

Ketcham & McDougall Mfg., Maiden Lane, New York, manufactured a pin-on holder in gold, silver, gun metal, rolled gold or black and white enamel. Small round pin-holders with a retractable chain were patented in 1915.

SQUARE-CUT STONE

Another design cut for gems.

STERLING

A British term referring to the highest standard of silver which has a fixed standard of purity: 925 parts of silver/75 parts copper.

The word originated with immigrant Germans who came across the Channel to England. They settled in a geographic area from which they took the name "Easterlings". Jewelers by trade, they were called upon to refine silver for coinage, and in 1343 the first two letters were dropped from the word "Easterling", resulting in the nomenclature: "sterling". It denotes the highest purity of silver. *All British sterling is hallmarked.*

Sterling silver, besides being utilized for conventional and *familiar* pieces of jewelry, was also produced as: veil clasps, ornamentation for elastic garters, ornately executed sash slides and buckles, additional trimmings for silk and *grosgrain* belts, hat marks, folding pocket combs, key rings, umbrella straps, bag or trunk checks, belt buckles and slides, ladies' hat-band buckles, armlets or garters, and frames for purses and bags.

STICKPIN (TIE PIN, SCARF PIN, ASCOT PIN)

Edwardians made more frequent use of jewels in men's neckwear because of the popularity of the wide-tie which could be beautifully accented by stickpins.

From approximately 1870 into the 20th Century, men and women of carriage wore stickpins in their hunting stock, scarves, or cravats; many were stylized forms of the riding crop, the fox, horses head, or a hunting dog. It was in the Edwardian Era that the jeweler's imagination soared, providing today's collector with innumerable miniature works of art conceived in the ornament atop the stickpin.

Many prize stickpins have been converted into charms or brooches since stickpins have been outmoded.

Stickpins were set with pearls, turquoise, diamonds, opals, rubies, amethysts, moonstone, coral, and even bezel-set hard-backed beetles. There were also their counterpart in glass or paste.

In 1893, stickpins were called *tie clasps* or *scarf holders.*

STRASS (or called *STRASSER)*

Brilliant lead glass perfected by Josef Strass for whom it was named. It is used in creating artificial gems or gemstones.

STUDS (also see SLEEVE BUTTONS)

Studs for men were usually of gold front and a rolled plate button-back. The small section on the front of the stud was very finely engraved or polished. Some were set with brilliants or garnets, some had enamel tops with the *fleur-de-lis* motif, inlays, Roman gold finish, etc.

They were usually sold in sets of three which were worn to the front with the end of the button-back inserted into the *inside* of the shirtwaist.

On July 30, 1872, a patent was taken out for a "separable stud", an ingenious device by H.A. & Co. The stud had a little squeeze-button-spring at the back which could separate the decorative front from the back and, therefore, could be used interchangeably with various types of decorative fronts such as, silver, *fleur-de-lis,* engraved, satin finish, Roman gold, French enamel. For the first time, the stud was shown in shapes such as square front or cube, rather than the usual round shape. Sold in sets of three they fitted into the hard, tuxfront of the shirt. The decade 1860-1870 is when studs appeared for the stiffbosomed shirts which became fashionable after the frills had vanished. Stiff shirts buttoned at the back and ornamental studs were actually for ornamental purposes rather than closure.

SWIVEL (or TONGUE CLIP)

A prong-snap connector which is mounted in a movable part, then joined by a hook-ring which is connected to the ends of watch chains into which the watch is snapped and hung.

SWIZZLE STICK

A vanity conceit carried by both men and women before the turn-of-the-century, but more often by the former. It was in demand with the introduction of sea-going passenger ships.

The swizzel stick entended into an umbrella of fine wires which were then swirled in a glass of champagne to reduce the carbonation. In reducing the carbonating bubbles, champagne becomes a white wine which is more easily digestible thus reducing the cause of sea-sickness.

It was considered a gentlemanly practice to take a swizzle stick, (often worn on a long chain and stored in the pocket), and use the extended swizzle by swishing it in the beverage before offering it to a lady.

It not only prevented sea-sickness, but avoided "spotting" powder or rouge. In yesteryear, of which we speak, heavy loose powdering was available unlike the solid-cake of powder manufactured today. In addition, swizzle sticks, by reducing carbonation, lessoned the chances of a lady belching in "polite society".

Swizzle sticks are still being manufactured by Tiffany & Co. but are worn more as a fad or fancy.

SYNTHETIC

The term differs from *imitation*. *Synthetic* stones are created by man's intelligent application of the chemicals which *nature* has produced through *natural* means. When referring to synthetic gems or gemstones, we also refer to the recent developments of man-made diamonds from pure carbon and the *Chatham* emeralds which are a synthetic speeding-up process of obtaining emeralds. In the art of synthesizing, man attempts to *duplicate* nature, whereas in chemical *imitations*, man seeks to merely *imitate* nature.

Doublets and triplets are stones consisting of two or more layers of material which are adhered to the top layer of a genuine stone. If one were to remove a doublet, triplet, or quadruplet from its setting and look at it from the side, the materials can be seen where they wre glued together. Ordinarily, a fine paste or a glass substance is glued to the genuine stone which makes the gem appear larger. This process is not considered either synthetic or imitation.

A fine example of man's ingenuity for creating a *synthetic* product is the cultured pearl, which is produced by man creating an "unnatural" irritation within the oyster's shell. Technically, a cultured pearl could be called synthetic, but since it is not "manufactured" by man but is rather produced by the workings of nature, it is called cultured.

With man harnessing the atom, and with more understanding of the workings of the configuration of atoms, it is not too far reaching to suppose that some day many, if not all, gems will be synthetically as well as naturally produced.

TIARA, - tĭ-ä´-ä

The word is derived from a Royal Persian headdress but is now accepted as any decorative jeweled or flowered headband or semi-circle worn by women for formal wear. The difference between a *tiara* and a diadem is that the latter is worn as a symbol of regal power or a crown of dignity.

TIE PIN (see STICKPIN)

The term is synonymous with stickpin. However, by 1900, the tie pin or cravat pin was called a *tie holder*, which resembled a baby's bib holder except that it was larger and more ornate. The clasp worked similarly to that of the bib holder. The tie clasps or holders, (a term used interchangeably), were in all metals, many with raised polished edges, gray and Roman finish, satin finish, rose and other gold finishes. They were engraved, had bright bevelled edges, and were finished in colored enamels.

TOOTH PICKS (or TOOTHPICKS)
The pick itself was usually solid gold but it could come with Celluloid handles, a rolled gold barrel, or sheath made of stone. Many were beautifully engraved. Some of the more popular, besides being enameled or engraved, came in a lovely swirl or cable style. This is true of both toothpicks and another instrument with a triangular point at the end of the pick which was used for cleaning the nails.

TOPAZ
A gemstone with the characteristic color of yellow which varies from canary to deep orange. In natural form it consists of translucent or opaque masses, or transparent prismatic cyrstals found in white, greenish or bluish colors. When some specimens are heated, they become pink or red. A yellow variety of quartz, namely citrine, is sometimes called "false topaz".

TORTOISE SHELL (or TORTOISESHELL)
Yellowish-brown grained substance which is the hard-plate shell from the back of the tortoise. Imitation tortoise shell was manufactured from plastic. Sadler Bros., South Attleboro, Mass., made imitation *Tortoisene*. Tortoise was used primarily for combs and hair ornaments, as well as some fine jewelry.

TRADE-MARKS (see HALLMARKS)

TREMBLER (or TREMBLANT)
A spring or wire mounted to an ornament in order to cause motion. The action gives a "nodder" effect. When used in conjunction with stones set into a floral pattern mounted on coil or straight-wire springs, it creates a fascinating dance of light which is reflected from the moving gems.

TRIANGULAR CUT
A shape cut for gemstones.

VERMICELLI, -vûr-mĭ-sĕl-ĭ
Italian for "little worms", used to describe thin gold wire twisted in a decorative design which "squirms like tiny worms". *Vermicelli* is not to be confused with granule work.

VICTORIAN ERA (1837-1901)
The 64-year reign of Queen Victoria, during which there were vast political and social changes, a rapid growth of industrialization, but a retention of strict moral rules and decorum which were challenged during the last half of her reign. "Victorian" now implies a "straight-laced, old-fashioned" approach to both morals and standards. The Victorian Era was, in fact, a time of great change from the Dark Ages to an age of enlightenment.

VINAIGRETTE, - vĭn-ā-grĕt′
A small conceit usually executed in gold or silver, with perforations on the top for holding aromatic vinegar, smelling salts, etc.

WAX-BEAD PEARLS (also see PEARLS)

Man-made pearls from the Bohemian area which were shipped by the ton to fashionable Paris and London and were utilized in hair and dress decorations as well as for jewelry. These imitation pearls had a wax-bead base, covered by a glass luster or by glass that had been irized.

WATCHES and WRIST WATCHES

Manufacturers of watches before the turn-of-the-century are written about in many fine volumes. Some of the more interesting places to find and identify a watch in your own possession would be in the catalogues of the period. There you will find not only replicas but exact descriptions, right down to the jewels in the setting, the type balance, the hair-spring, and the compensation-balance. Drawings show exposed pallets and the regulators. In other words, the entire stem-wind movements are minutely diagrammed as well as the cases to fit the movements.

One will be amazed at the ingenuity of design: the escalloped cases, many of them with rosette centers, others with a great deal of *vermicelli* work and raised ornamentation. The escalloped edge and the pastry or pie-crust shapes are very collectible. Besides the shapes of pastry shell or escalloped shells, which looked very much like the scalloped shell of the sea, there is the engraver's art to be admired.

There are many books on the subject and the reader is urged to research them. However, the reader should also venture into the many old catalogues which provide enlarged drawings or engravings of the innerworks of watch movements as well as the outer cases which include hunting cases and the simple bezel cases.

Both men's and women's watches were offered as premiums for selling various merchandise which began to appear in the home publications or magazines. Watches were exchanged for "one day's work" by boys and girls selling "1½ dozen packages of BLUEING . . .", an early bleaching agent. The premium offered was a nickle-plated watch. The same nickel-plated watch which had been offered to boys and girls for "a few hours work" was also offered for selling *Alpine Perfume*.

A *"beautiful gold-filled watch, stem-wind, stem-set, engraved, with a genuine American movement, warranted for two years"*, was offered to ladies selling "Beauty Pins" at *"5¢ each (regular price 10¢)"*. According to the advertisement, *"every lady and girl in the land needs several beauty pins"*. Over one million of these small beauty pins were selling per month by the Ladies Pin Co. of Chicago.

In reviewing several catalogues in which advertisements appeared for these premiums, it seems that the *fleur-de-lis* watch *pin* was the most popular offering with the lapel timepieces for ladies.

Protective cases made of either German silver, gun metal color alloys, or metallic gold colors, were used to protect a fine engraved precious gold or sterling silver cases which were to be worn by men as their "Sunday best". The protective cases enclosed the watch and prevented scratching, abrasions, or breakage during the daily work-a-day routine. Protective cases for women were more often made of tortoise shell.

Ladies' watches were smaller replicas of men's watches and were worn on *chatelaines* or with a watch pin.

Up until WWI, the pocket watch and the decorative lapel watch were fashionable, but with the wearing of military uniforms and with women attending factory work in clothing untypical of that worn in the past, both sexes adopted the wrist watch first initiated in the British army.

From 1910-1920, ladies' wrist watches were called *bracelet watch* and were convertible as a pin or as a bracelet. Wrist watches that were first introduced for women, had a crochet wrist band of fine crochet thread.

From 1920-1930, there were very stylish *Art Deco* flat, evening watches for men, worn with evening dress and without a chain. They were merely slipped into the vest pocket. Some of the flat watches for men held a combination cigar cutter.

In 1913, Ingersoll Watch Co. advertised "Horse Timers" and "Football Timers" with *Second Hands*. The Ingersoll Watch Co.'s slogan was *"The Watch That Made the Dollar Famous"*. The dollar watch was called "Yankee".

For historical information, serial numbers, and dates of American watches, write to: The National Association of Watch & Clock Collectors, P.O. Box 33, Columbia, Pa.

WEDGWOOD

Josiah Wedgwood, artist and potter, entered into partnership with Thomas Bentley, a manufacturer of porcelain, to form the English firm of Wedgwood in production of jasper wares. The production included jewelry, and was primarily in shades of blues and whites or green with white, depicting mythological figures in relief. The Wedgwood Company produced rings, cuff links, pendants, tie bars, barretts, and hundreds of cameos.

ZIRCON

A transparent variety of crystals which come in many colors such as yellow, brown, red, pink, etc., often used in birthstone rings as alternates for precious gems or gemstones.

ZIRCON-CUT

Similar to faceted rose-cut diamonds.

SECTION 4

CROSS-REFERENCE INDEX

CROSS-REFERENCE INDEX

SUBJECT	PLATE(S)

SECTION 5

BIBLIOGRAPHY
and
ACKNOWLEDGEMENTS

BIBLIOGRAPHY

ARTICLES

BAKER, STANLEY L., *"Collecting Art Deco"*, The Antique Trader, Dubuque, Iowa. (Dec. 10, 1974)

BUCK, J.H., *"Historical Sketch of Makers' Marks and Early American Legislation as to Silver"*, The Jewelers' Circular Publishing Company, New York. (1896)

"EARLY PLASTIC JEWELRY", Eleanor Gordon and Jean Nerenberg, The Antique Trader, Dubuque, Iowa. (Nov. 26, 1974)

FARHOLT, F.W., *"Marks of Gold and Silversmiths"*, Art Journal, London. (1855).

PATON, JAMES, *"Pins"*, Corporation Galleries of Art, Glasgow, Scotland. (1878)

BOOKS

"ART NOUVEAU JEWELRY & FANS", Gabriel Mourey, Aymer Vallance, et al., Dover Publications, New York. (1973)

BAINRIDGE, HENRY CHARLES, *"Peter Carl Faberge"*, The Hamlyn Publishing Group, Inc., London. (1966)

BAKER, LILLIAN, *"The Collector's Encyclopedia of Hatpins and Hatpin Holders"*, Collector Books, Paducah, Ky. (1976)

BAUER, DR. JAROSLAV, *"A Field Guide in Color to Minerals, Rocks and Precious Stones"*, Octopus Books, London. (1974)

BRADFORD, ERNLE, *"English Victorian Jewellery"*, Country Life Limited, London, *Four Centuries of European Jewellery"*, Hamlyn House, England. (1967)

BURGESS, F.W., *"Antique Jewelry & Trinkets"*. Tudor Publishing Company, New York. (1962)

CURRAN, MONA, *"Collecting Antique Jewelry"*, Emerson Books, Inc. (1963)

EVANS, JOAN, *"A History of Jewelry 1100-1870"*, Faber and Faber, London. (1953)

FALKINER, RICHARD, *"Investing in Antique Jewelry"*, Clarkson N. Potter, Inc., N.Y. (1968)

FLOWER, MARGARET, *"Victorian Jewellery"*, Cassell. (1951)

FREGNAC, CLAUDE, *"Jewelry From the Renaissance to Art Nouveau"*, G.P. Putnam's Sons, N.Y. (1965)

GERE, CHARLOTTE, *"Victorian Jewelry Design"*, Henry Regnery Company, Chicago. (1972)

GOLDEMBERG, ROSE LEIMAN, *"Antique Jewelry: A Practical and Passionate Guide"*, Crown Publishers Inc., N.Y. (1976)

HEINIGER, ERNST A. and JEAN, *"The Great Book of Jewels"*, New York Graphic Society, Ltd., Boston. (1974)

HERZBERG, MAX J., *"Myths and Their Meaning"*, Allyn & Bacon Inc., (1955)

HORNUNG, CLARENCE P., *"A Source Book of Antiques and Jewelry Designs"*, George Braziller, N.Y. (1963)

HUGHES, GRAHAM, *"Jewelry"*, E.P. Dutton and Co., N.Y. (1966);
"Modern Jewelry". Crown Publishers, Inc., N.Y. (1963);
"The Art of Jewelry", The Viking Press, N.Y., (1972)

"JABLONEC COSTUME JEWELRY -- AN HISTORICAL OUTLINE", Stanislav Urban and Zuzana Pestova, Museum of Glassware and Costume Jewelry, Jablonec, Orbis, Prague, Czech.

KOCH, ROBERT, *"Louis C. Tiffany, Rebel in Glass"*. Crown Publishers, N.Y. (1964)

KUNZ, GEORGE FREDERICK, *"The Curious Lure of Precious Stones"*, J.B. Lippincott Company, Phila., Pa. (1913)

LALIQUE, MARC ET MARIE-CLAUDE, *"Lalique Par Lalique"*, copyright *Societe Lalique, Paris, 1977.*

LAVER, JAMES, *"Victoriana"*, Hawthorn Books, Inc., N.Y. (1967)

LEWIS, M. D. S., *"Antique Paste Jewellery"*, Boston Book and Art, Publisher, Boston, Mass. (1970)

McCLINTON, KATHERINE MORRISON, *"Lalique for Collectors"*, Charles Scribner's Sons, N.Y. (1975)

MENTEN, THEODORE, "The Art Deco Style", Dover Publications, Inc., N.Y. (1972)
MEYER, FRANZ SALES, "The Handbook of Ornament", Wilcox & Follett Co. (1945)
SCHMUTZLER, ROBERT, "Art Nouveau", Harry N. Abrams, Inc., N.Y. (1962)
STEINGRABER, ERICH, "Antique Jewelry", Frederick A. Praeger, N.Y. (1957)
"THE STORY OF JEWELRY", Marcus Baerwald and Tom Mahoney, Abelard-Schuman, London. (1960)
"TRADE-MARKS OF THE JEWELRY AND KINDRED TRADES", The Jewelers' Circular Publishing Company, 11 John Street, New York. (1915)
"VICTORIAN SENTIMENTAL JEWELLERY", Diana Cooper and Norman Battershill, A.S. Barnes & Co., Inc., Cranbury, N.J. (1973)
WALKUP, Dr. Fairfax P., "Dressing the Part", F.S. Crofts & Co., New York. (1947)
WEINSTEIN, MICHAEL, "The World of Jewel Stones", Sheridan House, Inc., N.Y. (1958)
WILCOX, R. TURNER, "The Mode in Hats and Headdress, Including Hair Styles, Cosmetics, and Jewelry", Charles Scribner's Sons. (1959)

CATALOGUES

B.F. NORRIS, Alister & Co., 1893 Annual Catalogue, Chicago, Ill.
E.V. RODDIN & COMPANY, 1895 Catalogue, American Historical Catalog Collection, The Pyne Press, Princeton, N.J.
MERMOD & JACCARD JEWELRY CO. CATALOGUE, (Circa 1890), St. Louis, Mo.
MONTGOMERY & CO., "Fall & Winter 1894-97 Catalog & Buyer's Guide", edited by Joseph J. Schroeder, Jr., Follett Publishing Company, Chicago/New York, Copyright 1970 by The Gun Digest Company, Northfield, Ill. 60093.
O & Y CO. CATALOGUE, 1913.
SEARS, ROEBUCK & CO., CATALOGUES (1894-1913)
"THE CRYSTAL PALACE EXHIBITION ILLUSTRATED CATALOGUE, LONDON 1851", with new introduction by John Gloag, F.S.A., DOVER PUBLICATIONS, INC., N.Y.
THE NEW YORK JEWELER ILLUSTRATED ANNUAL CATALOGUE, S.F.M. Co., 1899

MAGAZINES

COUNTRY LIFE IN AMERICA (May 1913)
GODEY'S LADY'S BOOK AND MAGAZINE, Phila., Pa.,: (Feb. 1853, Dec. 1853, Nov. 1858, May 1860, Aug. 1874)
HARPER'S BAZAAR, (March 1873, March 1900)
JEWELERS CIRCULAR WEEKLY, (1913)
LADIES HOME COMPANION, (1897, 1901, 1906)
LADIES' HOME JOURNAL, (June 1916, Sept. 1931)
MODERN JEWELER, Hurst House, Inc., Kansas City, Mo. (Mar. 1977)
SCRIBNER'S MONTHLY, (1878)
THE DELINEATOR, (Feb. & Mar. 1900, July & Oct. 1901, Nov. 1902)
WOMAN'S HOME COMPANION, (Sept. 1910)

PERIODICALS

AMERICAN COLLECTOR   ANTIQUE MONTHLY
ANTIQUE TRADER   COLLECTORS NEWS
                KOVEL'S MONTHLY NEWSLETTER

OTHER SOURCES

ACQUIRE MAGAZINE   THE MAGAZINE ANTIQUES
        THE CREAKING ROCKER, (Centinela Antiquers monthly newsletter)

ACKNOWLEDGEMENTS

My thanks and gratitude to all those whose encouragement helped make this book possible, and especially to:

ALLEN, Betty- for scouting old newspapers and journals and sending me the clippings on jewlery.

BIDDLE, Jenny- who trusted me on "face value" with half her showcase of jewelry from Cape Cottage Antiques.

HENDRIX, Susan- who searched her collection of old magazines for information articles on jewelry.

FRANK, Vera- who lent her forty-year experience in gems and jewelry, and with her expertise set the guidelines for pricing.

HARRISON, Nat- of Dena Jewelers, who was always ready to answer questions or to find another expert or source who could; and for his friendship and confidence in my work.

HAUPTMAN, Joyce- my cordial, cooperative, effecient Secretary without whose help the manuscript would have taken ages to complete.

OLSEN, Ginny- of Ginny's Antiques, Et Cetera, for her enthusiasm and patience.

OTT, Rita- for her enthusiasm and for sharing tidbits of information which aided research and the project as a whole.

PEERY, Delma- of Wind Bells Cottage Antiques, for her confidence, time, and wisdom.

PIERCE, Shirlee- my totally efficient statistical typist and clerical worker without whose help there would be no meeting of deadlines.

SCHROEDER, Bill and Meredith- my publishers, without whose confidence, pattience, understanding, financial and moral support, no jewelry book could be realized.

STAMBOOK, R. E.- my photographer, who dragged his equipment the many miles from his residence to mine, over a period of months, in order to take the superb color plates for this book. Randy, who waited with infinite patience as the author arranged the jewelry plate layouts, then re-arranged, and re-arranged, again and again and again . . .he, never complaining, always smiling, aways, encouraging.

VAUGHT, Carolyn- who made her collection of priceless books and catalogues available to me, and for so freely sharing her knowledge of the subject.

WEBSTER, Hildegard- buyer for One-of-a-Kind Shop, Disneyland, who (with her associates), enabled me to photograph jewelry and jewelled accessories available to the buying public.

WRENCH, A.B.- Vice President, Caroline Emmons Div., C.H. Stuart and Company, Incorporated, Newark, New York State, for his spirited correspondence.

ZIMMERMAN, Jean- Asst. to the Director, Museum of Art, Rhode Island School of Design, Providence, R.I., for her helpful correspondence.

And to my jewel of a husband, who tolerates even when he doesn't understand the "mysterious moments and drives" in a writer's life.

To all those persons who made it possible for me to present their Heirloom pieces, Collections, or who removed jewelry from safes and shop showcases, entrusting me with the responsiblity and care of same -- my warmest thanks for your confidence and friendship without which this book could not have gone to press.

SECTION 6

JEWELRY COLLECTIONS REPRESENTED

THE JEWELRY COLLECTIONS REPRESENTED
IN THIS BOOK:

Louise Alexander

Antiques From Alota

Virginia Archer

George Riley Baker

Lillian Baker

Genevieve Barlow

Jenny Biddle,
   (Cape Cottage Antiques)

Joyce Cook

Disneyland, One-Of-A-Kind-Shop

Disneyland, Silver Shop

Vera Frank

Ann and Diane Fries

Ginny's Antiques, Et Cetera

Sherry Goldwasser

Juel Griesman

N. Harrison, (Dena Jewelers)

Sybel Heller

Lt. Com. (Ret.) & Mrs. Robert
   F. Henning

Manila Hoeck

Penelope Kastigir

Aldea Lambert

Bernice MacDonough

Virginia McCurdy

Ralph and Louise Majors

Renee Marshall

George W. Mills III

Collette Nance

Delma Peery,
   (Wind Bells Cottage Ant.)

Joyce Roth

Mrs. Ronald E. Schemm

Chris Skellington

Stells Tarr

Connie Taylor

Polly Toombs

Carolyn Vaught

Teresa Warren

Western Costume Co., (Los Angeles)

Virginia Whittier

AND ANONYMOUS COLLECTIONS